D1685121

Resound

seven stories, one sound

Resound Church

This book was written for the express purpose of conveying the love and mercy of Jesus Christ. The statements in this book are substantially true; however, names and minor details have been changed to protect people and situations from accusation or incrimination.

All Scripture quotations, unless otherwise noted, are taken from the New International Version Copyright 1973, 1987, 1984 by International Bible Society.

Published in Beaverton, Oregon, by Good Catch Publishing.
www.goodcatchpublishing.com
V1.1

Printed in the United States of America

Table of Contents

Acknowledgements 9

Introduction 13

1 An Answer to Pain 15

2 Running Shoes 43

3 The Unexpected Gift 73

4 647 101

5 Awakening 115

6 Yellow Brick Roads 141

7 Scrum 173

Conclusion 199

Acknowledgements

I would like to thank Pastor Luke Reid for his vision for this book, Nathan Lindley for the hard work, prayer and faith he put into this book to make it a reality and the people of Resound Church for their boldness and vulnerability in telling the stories in this compilation of real-life stories.

This book would not have been published without the amazing efforts of our project manager and editor, Marla Lindstrom Benroth. Her untiring resolve pushed this project forward and turned it into a stunning victory. Thank you for your great fortitude and diligence. Deep thanks to our incredible Editor in Chief, Michelle Cuthrell, for all the amazing work that she does. I would also like to thank our invaluable proofreader, Melody Davis, for the focus and energy she has put into perfecting our words.

Lastly, I want to extend our gratitude to the creative and very talented Alissa Reid, who designed the cover for *Resound: Seven Stories, One Sound.*

Daren Lindley
President and CEO
Good Catch Publishing

The book you are about to read
is a compilation of authentic life stories.
The facts are true, and the events are real.
These storytellers have dealt with crisis, tragedy, abuse
and neglect and have shared their most private moments,
mess-ups and hang-ups in order for others to learn and
grow from them. In order to protect the identities of those
involved in their pasts, the names and details of some
storytellers have been withheld or changed.

Introduction

What do you do when life is careening out of control? When addiction has overtaken you or abuse chained you with fear? Is depression escapable? Will relationships ever be healthy again? Are we destined to dissolve into an abyss of sorrow? Or will the sunlight of happiness ever return?

Your life can change. It is possible to become a new person. The seven stories you are about to read prove that people right here in our town have stopped dying and started living. Whether they've been beaten by abuse, broken promises, shattered dreams or suffocating addictions, the resounding answer is, "Yes! You can become a new person." The potential to break free from gloom and into a bright future awaits you.

Expect inspiration, hope and transformation! As you walk through the pages of this book with fellow Portlanders, you will not only find riveting accounts of their hardships; you will learn the secrets that brought about their breakthrough. These people are no longer living in the shadows of yesterday; they are thriving with a sense of mission and purpose TODAY.

May these stories inspire you to do the same.

An Answer to Pain
The Story of Thomas
Written by Lucy Phillips

The evening with Julia and her family was going nicely. We'd eaten dinner, then gathered in the living room to watch the local news on TV. I perched by the fireplace, and her dad settled into a comfortable chair. I liked this girl a lot.

Thankfully, I had already listened to a news report earlier that day, and I had a good idea of what was coming on TV that night.

My best friend, the one who had known me since childhood, had called me on my cell phone to warn me, but I already knew.

"Are you listening to this stuff?" he asked, telling me to turn on the radio. What I heard made me cringe all over again.

Julia's family and I watched as the television broadcaster announced that a Portland man and his co-conspirators allegedly had set off a bomb in a pornography store — as a decoy for the police while they robbed a bank. My former stepfather's bearded face loomed large on the television screen. He also was accused of plotting to blow up a government building with a fellow militant and was charged with growing marijuana.

I looked down at my feet. "That's my mom's second husband," I mumbled. I hoped I'd seen the last of Dieter when my mom finally divorced him, but he and his radical friends kept showing up in the media. My family recently had learned that Dieter, who by this time had become a prominent conspiracy theorist, was associated with the Army of God, a Christian anti-abortion terrorist group that had been linked to assassinations of people who performed abortions and bombings of abortion clinics. The FBI would soon pay my mom a visit to question her about Dieter.

My future father-in-law looked at the TV and then looked back at me.

"Huh," he said, nodding his head in wonderment.

I couldn't help but wonder, too. How could one man cause so much pain?

❧❧❧

Our move to Portland, Oregon, in 1984 wasn't easy on my mom. I was a baby when she left my dad, who was addicted to the morphine he took for pain from surgeries to correct injuries he received in a car crash. She found a full-time teaching job in Portland, and for the first time, she and I were on our own.

The day I sat on the yellowed linoleum in our kitchen and watched her cry is clear in my memory. As a toddler, I couldn't provide much comfort to my sweet, lonely mom.

She braced her hands against her lower back, which had been aching from all the weight she had gained recently.

An Answer to Pain

Mom was alone in a new city and uncomfortably overweight. The future was not looking bright for her or for us.

಄಄಄

Then, she met Dieter.

Dieter was a fledgling Christian author who my mom had come across briefly through a dating service and then reconnected with at a Bill Gothard youth seminar. He had bushy black hair and a thick beard, and his intense blue eyes matched the intensity of his personality. Dieter was working on exposing the fallacies of Jehovah's Witnesses and Freemasons.

He especially knew a lot about Jehovah's Witnesses, as he recently had been married to one and had a son with her. His concerns about his wife's religion became so great, he told my mom, that he kidnapped his son to rescue him from his mother.

Dieter went to jail for taking the boy, but he assured Mom that he was only trying to protect him.

Mom thought Dieter was cute, but she wasn't sure about his German surname — she didn't want to be stuck with it for the rest of her life. She waffled over whether to date him, and she almost called it off because of his financial immaturity.

Despite the distrust my grandmother and other family members felt for Dieter, my mom pushed aside her uneasiness and married him in 1986 when I was 5 years old. They had been together less than a year.

It was obvious that Dieter was brilliant. He was full of ideas, and he spent hours at his desk in our house typing manuscripts that he self-published into books the thickness of the *Yellow Pages*. If he wasn't writing, he was at Kinko's making copies of his books and papers.

I started to call Dieter "Dad," as he was the only father figure I'd known. We wrestled and played basketball sometimes, but something always felt off with him. For the most part, we were a regular family. Mom worked full time as a teacher to support us financially. We had family fun nights on Fridays, but that petered out as Dieter's writing hours became stranger and stranger.

❧❧❧

While Dieter had a group of friends who shared his ideas about conspiracies and government interference, he was just as willing to share his unabridged beliefs with me.

I watched a lot of TV when I was home with Dieter, and a popular Time-Life commercial for a series of books called *Mysteries of the Unknown* terrified me. Black and white drawings of alien heads filled the screen as a whispery man's voice wondered if they were real. A man floated in a dimly lit forest for 34 seconds. Was he suspended by an unseen force?

The pyramids, Stonehenge and a hand surrounded by a white aura flashed on the TV. "Is there a world more remarkable than we can ever imagine?" the narrator asked.

An Answer to Pain

The aliens' menacing black eyes and their upside-down triangle-shaped heads were burned into my mind.

Dieter was working at home, as usual, so I slowly walked to his desk to ask him about the aliens. I was hoping for the best-case scenario: a comforting hug like the mom in the Time-Life commercial gives her little girl when she's scared of the unknown.

"Are aliens from other planets real?" I asked Dieter, hoping for at least a solid, "No, son, that's just a commercial to sell books."

He swiveled around in his chair, his ice-blue eyes boring into me. He leaned forward so that his elbows rested on his knees.

"Thomas, that commercial isn't correct." My shoulders relaxed in relief. "Did it say that aliens came from other planets or other worlds?"

"Yes." I nodded eagerly.

"Aliens don't come from outer space. They live here on earth. Have you ever heard of reptilian entities? Let me tell you how they got here. Many years ago, fallen angels, who are demons, mated with humans and animals, and their offspring are what people would call aliens. This was before the time of Noah. Do you remember that story from Sunday school?"

This was not the answer I was looking for. Dieter continued, talking to me as if I were an adult at one of his seminars.

"In order to preserve life, God brought an end to the world and destroyed these genetic mutations. This was the flood described in the Bible. But it didn't wipe out all of the demons, who have again mated with humans. Today we have beings walking around who are a mixture of demons and flesh and blood.

"They look like humans, but you can tell they are so-called aliens by their reptilian eyes, which have diamond-shaped pupils like snakes and lizards. A psychologist I know has seen hundreds of people with eyes like this."

I backed away from Dieter, even more frightened now that I knew that not only were aliens real, but they were here on earth and looked a lot like humans. For a long time, I carried that fear inside me.

∽∽∽

Life with Dieter became increasingly bizarre. Instead of watching *Barney* videos, Dieter showed me homemade Christian tapes his friends sent him. In one music video, children sang about judgment and the end of the world. "Only 20 minutes to go," went the song's ominous refrain, sung by sickly sweet children's voices.

In the middle of the video, a long series of explosion scenes showed buildings collapsing and fires burning family pictures. During this rapture, the starring family goes to heaven.

As Christmas approached, the private Christian school I attended decorated for the holidays, and my friends excitedly talked about Christmas vacation plans and the presents they hoped would be under the tree.

An Answer to Pain

Their exuberance puzzled me.

"Don't you know the end times are coming?" I would implore. "Jesus is coming back this December. People are going to make us get bar codes implanted in our foreheads and wrists, and we have to refuse to do it. That's the mark of the beast, and you can't get to heaven if you have it.

"Guys, there's not going to be a Christmas this year. Or ever."

I was a regular school-kid prophet, parroting the information I was learning from Dieter, who was deeply embroiled in the 1988 end-times prophecies.

While grownups were buying into Dieter's theories and booking him to speak about the end of the world, my peers were giving me funny looks and walking away. Talking to them was like talking to a brick wall. They were looking forward to Christmas of 1988, but I quaked with fear.

কককক

God has been an important part of my life as long as I can remember. My grandmother and mother taught me about God and everything Jesus had done for me, and I loved God from an early age. With Dieter, though, our relationship with the church became strained. He had some issues with prominent Christian leaders.

One of those was evangelist Billy Graham, who brought his crusade to Portland in the early 1990s. The city was covered with posters and bumper stickers announcing the multi-day event, and our pastor encouraged the congregation to attend.

"That's all of the announcements I have for today," the pastor said from the pulpit one Sunday. "Have I missed anything?"

I sunk into the pew as Dieter stood up, scooted past the people in our row and walked to the front of the church. He addressed the congregation in his methodical, nonchalant voice.

"You may not realize this, but Billy Graham is not who you believe he is. He calls himself a Protestant, but he supports homosexuality, divorce and the Catholic church's worship of Mary. His deception, however, goes far beyond religious beliefs. He supports the one-world church, and in fact he was invited to Portland to lead this crusade by a National Council of Churches representative who is a new-age leader of the ecumenical movement.

"Billy Graham is often called the most respected man in America, but did you know he is a 33rd degree Freemason? His name has been dropped in casual conversation by other Freemasons, including a CIA agent. If you didn't know, Freemasonry is required to progress up the ranks of Satanism.

"I urge you not to support this Satan-worshiping, deceptive man, who is covering up a life of lies and deceit, or his crusade. Staying home is your best option."

The pastor stepped up behind Dieter, gently put his hand on my stepfather's back and ushered him back to his seat.

An Answer to Pain

"Thanks for that announcement, Dieter," the pastor said in a forced cheerful voice. "By the way, for anyone who would like to attend the Billy Graham crusade, the information will be available in the vestibule after the service."

❧❧❧

My brother Brian was born when I was 10 years old. Dieter was still writing, but his only contribution to the family income was an occasional $20 or $50 from book sales or a speaking engagement. When Dieter and my mom first married, he had a low-level government job working with computers that he soon quit to focus on his books and speaking. Since Dieter worked at home, he was expected to take care of Brian.

But Dieter was too obsessed with his ideas and his writing to bother with my infant brother. Brian inconvenienced Dieter, who was publishing newsletters for his followers and working on new books, and he kept childcare to the bare minimum. Dieter was sinking deeper into his personal mission to expose the secrets of Satanism and Satanic ritual abuse, and when he wasn't home working, he was traveling the country giving talks about how political leaders were either puppets unknowingly under mind control or people perpetuating mind control. Brian was a bother to him, and sometimes Dieter would spank Brian angrily if Brian interrupted his work.

Dieter often printed his material late at night, so he

liked to sleep during the day. That meant he needed Brian to nap as much as possible, so he would give him bottle after bottle to help him sleep, long after he should have been weaned to a Sippy cup. Eventually, some of Brian's baby teeth rotted.

A clunking noise startled me one day while I was reading in the basement, and I heard a piercing cry that I knew came from Brian. I looked up and saw my baby brother thumping down the stairs, bouncing off the steps on the way down.

"Brian!" I cried, jumping up from the couch. The stairs had metal edges, and I could just imagine his head slamming into one.

Just before he hit the concrete basement floor, I swept Brian into my arms, saving him from what could have been a serious injury. Brian bawled as I clutched him tightly, both of us frantic with fear and relief. Miraculously, he wasn't hurt. My anger boiled at Dieter's negligent parenting.

Not long after, when Mom and Dieter were divorcing, Brian was somehow able to muster the words, "You need to find a daddy who will take care of me." He couldn't have been more right.

≈ ≈ ≈

In the early 1990s, Dieter became obsessed with treating people who supposedly had suffered from Satanic ritualistic abuse. Many of them had Multiple Personality

An Answer to Pain

Disorder (MPD), and they came to our house to see Dieter, as would his growing circle of Christian conspiracy theorist friends. They would sit in our living room deep in conversations, and I overheard stories and snippets of conversation about setting fire to abortion clinics, resisting the government and exposing conspiracies.

We spent one evening with a man who had MPD who seemed perfectly normal. He was fun and talkative, and compared to Dieter's other friends, he seemed pretty rational.

Later that week when I got home from school, I pressed the button on the answering machine to listen to the messages. It was that man, calling repeatedly for my mom.

I hit delete 30 times. He had left message after message cussing my family out and calling my mom horrible names. I erased every single message so my mom wouldn't have to listen to those ugly words.

Inside, I seethed. I was taking care of my mom, protecting her from these voicemail messages, and where was Dieter? Why wasn't he contributing to our family's income when we were so worried about how we would pay the bills every month? Why was he friends with these people? Why was he spending so much time on those enormous books about Satanism that cost so much to print that he couldn't possibly have profited on their few sales?

My gentle, soft-spoken mother did not make good choices in men.

Resound

~~~~

With my mother's permission, I began exchanging letters with my real father, who had cleaned up his life and settled down in Texas. He had always been a good Christian man, but he had made some big mistakes over the years. My parents met when he was an adjunct professor at a Christian university and she was a student in the band there. They were both musical, as was I.

In the summer of 1993, Dieter, my mom, Brian and I went on a driving vacation across 14 states, including a stop in Texas to see my dad. He didn't look like the skinny, dark-haired man in a suit from our family pictures. Now, he was overweight with a crew cut.

We met him at Copperfield's Restaurant, but we were both so shy and quiet that we didn't really know how to talk to each other. Plus, Dieter was there, and his relentless "My Two Dads" jokes made any attempts at real conversation ridiculous and awkward.

As our lunch wrapped up, I fiddled with the little game on the table because I didn't know what else to do. Dad, who was wearing a back brace, leaned down on his way out so that he could speak to me privately.

"I love you," he said softly.

I looked down. I wanted to say "I love you" back, but I also wanted to be honest. I didn't really know this man. I said nothing.

About a year later when I walked into the house from school, Dieter directed me to their bedroom and told me I should talk to my mom. I found her sitting on the bed, crying. My dad had checked into the hospital for another back surgery that day, and he had died suddenly of a blood clot. My heart ached for my mom, who was so sad.

I went to school the next day, even though my parents said I could stay home to absorb the shocking news about my dad. I wanted to take my mind off what had happened. During recess, I jumped into a heated game of foursquare.

The red playground ball bounced in and out of my square, and I concentrated on making strategic hits so that I could move to the next square. As the ball slid off my fingertips, hot tears began streaming down my face, and the gravity of my dad's death hit me like a semi-truck. The ball rolled away, and I stood in my square, sobbing.

Not knowing what to do, I took off for the bathroom and shut myself in a stall. The tears didn't stop.

"Thomas, are you okay?" asked Ron, a good friend at school who had followed me into the bathroom. Ron's mom was single and a little odd, and we connected. "What's wrong?"

I lost my father just as I was getting to know him. That's what's wrong.

My sadness over my dad and my anger at Dieter blazed like two fires inside of me, extreme emotions I mostly kept bottled up because I had to take care of my mom and Brian. I had nowhere to direct my feelings, and they just burst out of me sometimes with no warning. One time, after Brian, who later was diagnosed with Asperger's Syndrome, had had a particularly bad night, I was so mad

Resound

I punched a post downstairs in our house and broke my hand.

∾∾∾∾

Dieter decided that a certain female patient he was treating for ritualistic abuse needed especially careful observation and intense treatment. He spent more and more time at her house until he was essentially living there. Her husband inexplicably moved into their garage to accommodate Dieter's deprogramming of his wife.

My family barely saw him anymore, and I liked it that way. It was easier to keep him tuned out.

We also were figuring out that Dieter and his friends were truly wacky, and the ones we liked were distancing themselves from him. Details came to light about his so-called Christian friends, such as the man who believed that God was some kind of electrical force. He and his wife had eight kids, and they were so poor that the children were starving. His wife left him. We learned another of Dieter's friends was beating his family. Dieter was surrounded by chaos.

My mom had tried to make this marriage work for years, and I was tired of the neglect and emotional strain we had to deal with.

Finally, I just spoke to her bluntly. Brian, who had just turned 3, stood by my side.

"You need to divorce Dieter and get away from him. You've given him enough chances. It's time for him to go."

An Answer to Pain

Thankfully, my mom actually agreed and made him move out. She had recently found a black box under her bed, and to her astonishment there were several fake IDs with Dieter's picture on them. That discovery, along with Dieter's new living arrangements, were too much for her to take.

Dieter, however, wasn't going to let her divorce him without a fight. The custody battle over Brian drug on for several years. He repeatedly charged my mom with slander in his newsletter, telling his subscribers that people had told him my mom was controlled by demons and had given her life to Satan.

My mom wanted to get a restraining order against Dieter, but it was hard to convince a judge to grant one based solely on my stepfather's weirdness. He hadn't done anything illegal to us.

One day, Dieter showed up at our house unannounced. I watched through the window as he climbed our front steps, and memories of him kidnapping his first son so many years ago flashed into my mind. A plan formulated for how I would defend Brian, who was still a little boy.

I opened the door a crack, Brian clinging to my legs.

"I have a present for your brother," Dieter said, holding out a bag.

"You're not supposed to be here."

Dieter leaned over to get a better look at Brian. "Your brother is acting weird."

"Don't talk to me like that. You're not supposed to be

here. You need to leave." This time, Dieter did hand me the gift and left.

Other visits didn't resolve as smoothly, such as the time he arrived for a supervised visit and took off with Brian while the chaperone was in the bathroom. He eventually brought my brother back, but it was yet another stressful incident in the draining and difficult divorce.

&~&~&~

Every summer, I went to Bible camp, and my last year of junior high was the last year I could go. Throughout the years with Dieter, I had not lost my connection with God. I had been baptized at a young age and gone to Christian private school most of my life. Most of the time, though, I stayed mad at Dieter and God.

One night after we had circled around the campfire, one of the counselors sat the boys down outside for an impromptu sermon. His steady voice punctuated the stillness of the campgrounds, and it also pierced my heart.

"God has forgiven us for everything we've done, and I mean everything," the counselor told us. "In the same way, we need to forgive people who have hurt us, even if they don't deserve it. If we don't, it's going to hurt us more than the other person."

I really thought about those words as we walked back to our cabins and climbed into our bunks. I was so angry at Dieter, but all of my anger wasn't hurting him at all. It was only hurting my family and me.

An Answer to Pain

The ceiling loomed only a few feet above me in my upper bunk. I stared into the darkness, praying.

God, I don't want to forgive Dieter, but I am going to.

If I couldn't forgive him in my heart, I would at least speak the words. "I forgive him," I whispered.

A weight lifted off me, and for the first time in my life, I physically felt God's presence. Years of anger dissipated into the night air.

I checked in with myself often the next day. *Am I still mad at Dieter? Is the anger still here?* The answer was no every time. The anger really disappeared, and it's still gone. At times I have been frustrated, but the rage that consumed me never returned. Over the years, I've learned that even though Dieter is a messed-up, hurtful person, God loves him just as much as he loves me. I've even prayed for him sometimes, and in a way I've loved him because God loves him.

❧❧❧

College didn't start well for me. I planned to be a shining light and a Christian presence on campus, but like so many other kids, I started drinking heavily almost right away. I slipped farther and farther away from God, partying, getting into impure relationships with girls and spending many nights drinking alone. The theater scene is very self-focused, and I was not immune to its allures.

A movie turned everything around for me, like flipping a switch. The plotline involved a drug dealer who

chooses drugs over his family. I made the connection —
my real dad had chosen morphine over my mom and me.
For the first time, I realized that my dad's choices had led
to a lot of anger and hurt in my life.

It was time for me to move on from my wild ways and
do something good.

During high school, I had sometimes led worship at
my church, but I didn't feel like I was in a place to be
leading anybody at this time. I decided that if someone
from church asked me to lead, I'd be a leader. Not long
after, a youth leader asked me to join the team.

While in college, I joined a group that prayed for the
kids every Monday, and my faith was set on fire like it had
never been before. My fellow leaders were passionate
followers of God, and their faith was infectious. I was
asked to join the youth leadership team and participated
in the youth meetings. At first I just made small talk with
the youth, but as I got to know them, my relationships
with them grew stronger. At the leadership meetings
where we joined together to pray for the youth, my faith
and passion grew.

I had decided this was not the time for a relationship,
but one Sunday morning, a bagel hanging out of my
mouth, I looked across the church and saw Julia.
Something quickened inside, and I knew this was the
woman God wanted me to pursue. We married in 2005. I
transferred to a local Bible college, and there I took classes
on preaching and the Bible. A youth pastor was mentoring
me, pouring life and wisdom into me. He was so cool and

An Answer to Pain

laidback, brilliant and challenging. *If I was like him,* I thought, *I could do ministry.*

But the pain of the world still weighed on me. I wondered how such bad things could happen. How do people deal with so much hurt?

Reading *The Brothers Karamazov* on a plane ride to Mississippi in 2006 didn't help. I'd also packed C.S. Lewis' *The Problem with Pain* in my bag, hoping to find some intellectual answers to my questions.

Pascagoula, Mississippi, was still reeling from the destruction wrought by Hurricane Katrina the year before, and our youth group traveled there to help with relief efforts. My ears were filled with amazing testimonies from the people we met: the woman who successfully rebuked in the name of Jesus the waves crashing into her house; the car that floodwaters carried out of a garage and somehow brought back in.

God had met these people in these hardest of times. When they hugged me, it was a sincere, serious hug. The unbearable pain and loss they shared had birthed an incredible community of Christian believers. They were passionate for God because life had left them no other choice.

I fell to my knees one night as we worshiped with our new community in Mississippi.

Your relationship with me is worth fighting for, God told me. My questions about pain lingered, but I now knew that I would keep seeking God until I had the answers.

Resound

❦❦❦

My mom was ready to find someone.

She joined Christian dating Web sites and met a man online who lived in Quebec. She assured me they were just friends and that they weren't going to rush into anything. I was eager for my mom to meet a companion, but this guy was in his 50s, and I thought it was odd that he had lived with his mom his whole life. When he came to Portland to visit her, he was open about his past struggles with alcohol.

Mom moved to Quebec and in with Dean and his mother, anyway. Even though it was a terrible situation, they got married and returned to Portland. Soon, Dean was drinking and continued acting strange.

One day I received a call at my office. Dean, who was a martial arts expert, had thrown Mom and Brian into a wall in a fit of anger. They were at the police station, covered in the chocolate milk Brian had been drinking.

Julia and I allowed Mom and Brian to move into our two-bedroom duplex, and it was cramped. The old anger and frustration returned. I so much wanted life to be good for my mom, and it just never happened. When I was a kid, I thought the world was dumping bad things on her. Now, I could see that many of those bad things came from her bad decisions. I was still mad, though, and distraught at my mom's pain. One night I opened a bottle of wine for Julia and me and then drank the whole bottle myself. I had long ago given up drinking, but my old bad habit resurfaced that night. With my interim youth pastor position ending, I struggled with whether I should go into full-time ministry. My mom's third messy divorce had shaken my confidence in whether I could tell people that God was good and they should follow him.

While I didn't feel as if I could stand in a pulpit and hold a place of authority in a church, I could still do what God had called me to do. Feeling empathy and serving others was more of what I was drawn to.

❧❧❧❧

Julia and I stumbled upon the perfect job for us: house parents for group homes for children in the foster care system. We moved to a small town in the mountains of Western North Carolina and into a house out in the country near a lake. It was beautiful, and almost every other family living there was Christian.

The man who served as recruiter and trainer at the group homes inspired me. He had a radical faith and a radical personality. He told amazing stories of foster parents showing the love of Christ to these kids, such as one about an ex-prison guard foster parent who ended up taking care of an 18-year-old autistic teenager who was unable even to bathe himself. The hulking guy would walk around our camp holding hands with the teenager. This struck me as such a sweet relationship.

In that town, our house was filled with girls, from infants to teenagers. Our days were so packed that at night

Resound

Julia and I would remember important things we'd forgotten to tell each other during the day, such as that one of our girls was cutting herself again. Before this job, I had gotten used to spending time with God throughout the day, and now I was praying on the run.

Sometimes I would sit on our porch, watch the sunset and think about all of the things I had seen and heard that day. Some of the girls who stayed with us had suffered terrible abuse, and most still dealt with the aftermath.

As my dog lay on the ground and chewed a stick, I pondered how these things could ruin someone's faith. I knew that just behind me inside the door, girls were running around and yelling profanities at each other. Surely they must have experienced terrible hurt before they came here.

One of these nights, I realized that God is bigger than all of this, no matter how messed up it was. God is still good, despite people's bad choices. God, I finally understood, was greater than our circumstances and our pain.

I thought about the amazing people who had mentored me. Dad and Dieter had been terrible examples, but God had provided many other men in my life who had loved me and shown me who God is. They took me to youth group events, mentored me, played music with me and read the Bible with me. God used the Christian community as part of the answer to pain.

Within a year, Julia and I had a son, and we were living in a house full of troubled girls. I turned into a papa bear.

An Answer to Pain

More than anything, I wanted my son to have an easier childhood than I did. I loved him so much, and when I realized how the chaos in our home could affect him, I became very protective.

We packed into a van to drive to church one Sunday, and the girls piled in around our infant son, who was strapped into his car seat. As usual, a few of the girls began acting up, probably because they weren't looking forward to sitting still through the church service.

Julia had worked hard to get one girl, who had been angry for several days, calmed down and into the vehicle. She handed the girl a notebook to draw in during church, and another girl slapped it out of her hand. The notebook sailed through the air and hit my son square in the face. He began to cry, and the girl jumped out of the van and took off, maybe out of guilt. Julia had to chase her.

I practically went into shock. All I was concerned about was my little boy, but I had to quickly secure him in the house and then track down Julia and the girl.

Our heart's desire had been to stay in North Carolina for a long time, but after the van incident, Julia and I felt like we couldn't guarantee our son's safety amid the behavior problems of the girls we were caring for. We knew this girl hadn't meant to hurt our son, but he was growing up in a situation where the chances were good he could be hurt unintentionally.

With great sadness, we left our jobs and our close Christian community after only a year and a half. This job had felt like our calling, but Julia had to do much of the work caring for the girls, and she was worn out. We returned to Portland.

❧❧❧

We moved in with Julia's parents, and I started looking for a job. After my time in North Carolina, I was ready for church ministry again.

One of the churches looking for worship musicians was Resound Church. I met Luke, the pastor, for coffee and talked about joining the worship team. There wasn't a paid position, but I couldn't shake the feeling that this church was where Julia and I needed to be. The excitement I'd felt about the group home job washed over me again.

Julia and I were one of the first couples from Portland to join Luke and his church-planting team, which had moved west from Iowa. They wanted their church to embrace creativity and love the area.

Resound Church was born from this group that first met in Luke's living room. My enthusiasm for this new endeavor was so great that I turned down a couple of offers to work at other churches, even though I desperately needed a job. I'd rather be playing the guitar for free at Resound.

❧❧❧

I took lame temp jobs to pay the bills, although it was never enough that we could move into our own place.

An Answer to Pain

When people asked me what I did for work, I would reply "customer service" or "I work for a temp agency." I kept the details about the call centers and the menial office jobs, the 40-minute commute each way, to myself.

I was driving so much to get to work that I didn't have time to exercise. I gained weight and was getting depressed. On Sundays, church would fill me with the excitement of hope, but the workweek drained it all out of me.

It was a far cry from my life as a radical Christian serving in the trenches with foster kids.

One temp job was particularly frustrating. My boss hadn't given me clear instructions on how to do the work, and every day just added up to more hours of aggravation.

I'm sorry, God, I prayed as I cruised through the traffic one day on my way home. *I want to do my best at this job. I want to excel in Jesus' name. I'm sorry, I'm sorry, I'm sorry...*

God answered.

You have nothing to be sorry about. I love you just the way you are.

I broke down crying right there in the car, tears blurring my vision. A new peace was planted in my soul. God loved me no matter what my job.

My next temp position turned into another office job with an end date, and I couldn't have been less excited. But here, I could excel, and the job became long-term work that paid enough for us to move to Hillsboro and closer to our new community at Resound Church.

Resound

The church had grown from nine people to 250. Julia and I could relax together in the evenings, and sometimes I thought about how I'd like to be involved in more intentional ministry.

But struggles with identity with my work lingered. Should I return to church work or find a job helping others through a nonprofit? Why do I sometimes end up in office jobs?

On a recent Sunday, I stood around after church talking with two guys who had played on the worship team that week. I felt a gentle tapping on my arm and looked down at a skinny kid with sandy-blond hair.

"I just felt like I was supposed to come up and pray for you," he told me. The kid was probably about 12, and I appreciated his boldness.

"That's awesome."

We sat side-by-side in some chairs, and he put his hand on me.

I closed my eyes as he sang softly and then spoke in a special prayer language. We sat together in silence for a while.

"I feel like there's something you've been sad about for a long time," he finally said. "I feel like God is telling me to tell you that he's going to fix it."

I had been so consumed with worries that God wasn't going to use me in ministry, and this child's prayer erased that longtime fear.

Now ministering in my family brings me indescribable joy. With my son and our baby on the way, I can replace the negative examples of fatherhood I grew up with and do everything in my power to share God's love with them. I'm looking for a job with a nonprofit organization where I can teach young people life skills that will help them avoid the family problems I experienced.

The simplicity of a child telling me that Sunday that God was going to "fix it" was exactly what I needed to hear. It's really that uncomplicated. My heavenly father can fix anything, including the thoughts in my head and the pain that had settled in my heart. Faith can be hard, and life can hurt. Ultimately, though, faith is something God wants for everybody, and because of that, it's simple.

Running Shoes
The Story of Sydney
Written by Karen Koczwara

I whirled around and frantically scanned the crowded room. Where on earth had my husband gone? One minute we'd been socializing, the next he had disappeared. I brushed past the crowd, a blur of swishy cocktail dresses, neckties and black suits, mumbling my apologies as I darted out the door.

Up ahead, I saw the tail of his coat, and both relief and anger washed over me.

"Tanner, what are you doing? I've been looking all over for you!" I stopped to catch my breath as my husband slipped into the elevator.

"I'm not feeling well," he replied, avoiding my eyes. "These social events … not really my thing."

"What do you mean, not your thing? You love parties!" I protested.

"I'd much rather just go somewhere quiet with you … please, can we get out of here?"

There we stood, me in my chic cocktail dress, him in a suit, the quintessential socialite couple in the middle of New York City. It was supposed to be a memorable night; an art gala I had looked forward to for weeks, cocktails, fancy hors d'oeuvres, a great view of Lower Manhattan and networking with some of New York's finest professionals. Yet my husband had darted out on me just moments after we'd walked in the door. It didn't make sense.

"Please, let's go." Tanner was almost pleading now, his eyes desperate and … was it … panicked? Why on earth was my social, charismatic, life-of-the-party husband suddenly acting so strange?

I slipped in the elevator, smoothing my beautiful dress as we made our descent. Deep in my gut, I knew something was wrong. It wasn't just tonight. It was a million other things that didn't add up. I'd tried to ignore them, told myself they couldn't be true. But that nagging sense that things just weren't right kept surfacing, waking me up at night, taking my breath away.

"You really look beautiful. Let's go somewhere quiet, just the two of us." Tanner took my hand, and I gingerly intertwined my fingers with his.

Though we stood just inches apart, close enough to feel each other's breath on our cheeks, I felt miles away from my husband, weighed down with a secret burden I could not share. I had to find out the truth.

I had to find out just who my husband was.

෨෨෨

Born and raised in a fourth-generation pastor's home, I had no reason to believe that life could be harsh. My older brother, younger sister and I grew up in a busy fast-paced home centered around church and lived a fairly idyllic childhood. Grateful for a positive upbringing, I

Running Shoes

always assumed my life would include ministry and that I would serve God for the rest of my life.

After graduating high school, I attended a couple universities on the west coast and landed at a private Christian liberal arts university in the greater Seattle area, where I completed my degree in Christian Education. The morning of my graduation, the president of the university singled me out in the sea of cap-and-gowned peers and pulled me out of line.

"God woke me up in the middle of the night to tell me that he would use you and open many doors in your life," he told me.

I had always hoped God would use me for great things, but to hear the president of the university confirm this was both humbling and amazing.

"Wow, thank you," I replied incredulously.

I loved the university so much that I pursued a career on campus as the campus ministry coordinator, planning services and activities for the students. I loved the job, loved the culture and loved my peers; at the time, I was completely content.

Two years after graduation, I led a group of students on a missions trip to Ensenada, Mexico. On our way back to our hotel in San Diego, the driver of our van had an anxiety attack, and I was forced to drive the van full of students. A guy I had just met, who happened to be speaking at a summer camp in Mexico, hopped in the van and offered to help me navigate my way back to the team hotel.

Resound

"I know my way around here pretty good, so why don't I take over?" he suggested. He introduced himself as Tanner, and within minutes, we were chatting away like old friends. Tanner was from Seattle as well; that was just one of the many things we discovered we had in common.

"Nice to meet you. Have a great rest of your trip!" I called out when we parted ways later that night. Guys were the last thing on my mind at that point, and the chances of ever seeing Tanner again were very slim. Though we had hit it off amazingly well, I chalked up the meeting to a pleasant acquaintance and kept my focus on the trip.

A few weeks later, back in Seattle, I happened to run into Tanner. Surprised, I said hello and went on my way. These casual encounters continued; I ran into Tanner several more times during the next few months. One evening, while dining out with friends, I heard someone call my name from across the restaurant.

"Hey, Sydney!" a warm, familiar voice rang out.

Before even looking up, I knew it was Tanner. He sauntered to the table and announced that we just so happened to be part of the same dinner party; as it turned out, we had mutual friends.

"Who is that guy?" my friend asked when we slipped out to the restroom.

"Oh, just someone I keep running into," I replied. "Seems nice enough."

"Cute, too. What would you say if he asked you out?"

I thought for a moment. "I guess I'd say yes. He's … interesting."

Running Shoes

At the end of the evening, Tanner asked for my e-mail to pass along some information he had that I wanted to forward to a friend.

I agreed to send it to him, and over the course of the following weeks, we e-mailed back and forth. It didn't take long for Tanner to make his intentions extremely clear: He wanted to pursue me.

"I haven't dated in seven years," Tanner told me. "I became a Christian in high school and have been focusing on God and other things ever since. I think you're the kind of girl I've been waiting for, Sydney."

I was flattered; every girl loves the thrill of being pursued. Cautious from previous relationships, I was hesitant to give my heart away. But so many things about Tanner attracted me to him; he was outgoing, charismatic, passionate about his faith, adventurous, a risk-taker and he had an entrepreneurial spirit. He wanted to use his gifts to help others in ministry and the nonprofit sector; God had confirmed that he would open doors for me someday, and I believed that perhaps Tanner was part of that grand plan.

Little did I know what that "grand plan" entailed.

వ∾వ∾వ

After dating for a year and a half, Tanner proposed to me. On a warm summer night in 2004, I married my dream man in a dream wedding, complete with all my closest friends and family and a night full of memories to last a lifetime. A blissful honeymoon followed, and I truly thought life could not get more perfect than it had.

A ministry position opened up at a church in Portland, and the executive pastoral team hired me on as director of volunteer and young professional ministries. Tanner kept his day job while volunteering as a speaker and leader at the same church. He spent much of his time working on his ever-changing business ventures; there was always a new one up his sleeve.

"I really think this one might be it," he said excitedly one night. "I've got this big project lined up on the Oregon coast, and it's gonna be huge."

I smiled. "I hope so, babe." I was used to listening to Tanner's grandiose ideas before bed every night, and I sincerely did hope that one of them would be "it." As the cautious one in the marriage, I kept us tethered to the ground while Tanner soared from one thing to the next. I remained supportive, cheerleading him on from the sidelines while he dreamed and plotted.

In the fall of 2005, we resigned our positions at the church. Tanner continued his business ventures while I prayed about what God might have in store for my career. I was a go-getter and knew I was made for more than sitting along the sidelines in life.

One day, Tanner came to me, a fresh gleam in his eye. "I know I keep saying this, babe, but this one is really it. This is huge. I am pulling together a pool of investors to buy a building on Wall Street in New York City … it's gonna be huge."

Running Shoes

"New York City? Wall Street, as in *the* Wall Street?" I asked, somewhat overwhelmed by the idea. A business venture on the Oregon coast was one thing, but New York City was, well, practically the financial axis of the world.

"Yup. The building is a historical landmark in downtown Manhattan. We are going to renovate the building into a boutique hotel, executive office spaces, high-end retail and fine dining establishments ... oh, man, it's gonna be crazy. We're gonna make lots of money and have tons to give back to churches, ministries and causes we believe in. Just trust me on this, okay?"

I stared at my husband, who was practically dancing around the room. He was always filled with enthusiasm, but I had never seen him this excited about something before. "Wow. Well, you know I trust you, Tanner. I look forward to seeing how all of this unfolds."

The next couple of years were a whirlwind, as Tanner flew back and forth to New York to pursue his new business venture. I stayed back in Portland, unemployed and still not sure where to go next in my own life. Knowing the New York business venture would eventually take us to the city full time, I tried to remain patient and offered my administrative support to him.

"I'm really good at keeping track of all the details," I reminded Tanner. "Why don't you let me take care of that side of things so you can focus more on the rest of the business?"

Tanner agreed initially, but he didn't divulge much information. When I persisted, he told me he couldn't share everything with me but insisted I trust him. "It's all gonna be amazing, babe. You'll see," he promised.

For Christmas 2006, we flew to New York to visit and scout out condos as we knew our move to the city was impending. I was enthralled by the bright lights, the dazzling stores and the hustle and bustle pace of the city. Tanner and I both agreed that it would be best if we moved to New York full time for a couple years; when the business was fully established, we could return to the West Coast. It sounded like an adventurous, exciting plan.

Two months before our big move, I found a huge stack of bills that had not been paid and confronted Tanner. "Why didn't you pay these?" I demanded. Money was supposedly not an issue; there was no reason for them to be sitting there still. "I thought you said you had taken care of everything."

"Don't worry about it. I got it all under control, remember?" Tanner said coolly.

I sighed and whipped out the checkbook. We were still newlyweds, trying to find our day-to-day rhythm and routine. These things would work themselves out in time. Or so I thought.

As we packed our things and made the big move across the country, my nerves rattled me a bit. *Just trust the Lord, and trust your husband,* my heart told me. *Everything is going to be okay.*

We narrowed our search for a condo down to three places, and we were thrilled when we settled on one on the Upper West Side of Manhattan overlooking the beautiful

Running Shoes

Hudson River. As the model condo in the new complex, it came completely furnished. Since we had taken only our basic belongings with us from Portland, the furniture was a huge blessing. My heart began to ease up, as I truly began to believe that God had led us to New York City and would provide for all our needs.

When I asked where money was coming from, Tanner always explained that several investors were funding the business, making it possible for things to get moving. I trusted him; it seemed like a logical agreement.

As the months passed, Tanner grew busier than ever. He flew to places like Europe, South America, Turks and Caicos, insisting the connections he had gained there would make his business very profitable someday. "I'd also really like to start a foundation from the funds that come in so we can impact others," he said excitedly.

I was on board with that; I sincerely hoped we could use the promised wealth to be a blessing to others and also keep focused on ministry, which had always been my first passion.

I had truly fallen in love with New York City, but as Tanner became increasingly busier, a deep loneliness settled into my heart. My life had always been full of supportive friends and family; now I found myself in a huge city filled with people, yet often times feeling more isolated than ever.

During his spare time, Tanner remained attentive to me, taking me to exciting places, exploring the city and wining and dining me at some of Manhattan's best restaurants. We communicated all day long, which kept me from feeling completely isolated. I convinced myself that our marriage was just as strong as ever.

I had no idea that my life was about to tragically unravel.

ৡ৵ৡ৵ৡ৵

I met a couple who became like family to me in the city. The husband, a successful entrepreneur, had worked with nonprofit organizations as a professional coach. He invited me to be a volunteer administrative coach on his team. Eager to use my administrative skills again, I hopped on board and poured myself into nonprofit companies, coaching people as they got their organizations off the ground. It felt good to be doing what God had created me to do once again.

One weekend, I attended a large company event that included several training sessions for the Christian coaching organization. We were grouped together with others and trained for personality profiling. As our session came to a close, one of the gentlemen in my group pulled me aside. "God has given me a word I'd like to share with you," he began.

I wondered if he'd tell me God had a great plan for my life. Instead he said, "Have you been struggling with self-doubt lately?"

Tears pricked my eyes, and I nodded slowly. "Yes." For the past several years, I had felt like I was floating around, bobbing from one thing to the next without a real sense of purpose. While I had once been self-confident, I had begun to feel lately that I was losing my identity.

"God has given you discernment, and he wants you to walk in that. Don't walk in self-doubt, and he will open doors for you."

The leaders stopped the session to pray for me right then and there. Tears I'd stored away now spilled down my cheeks as I thanked God for his word.

It wouldn't be long before I would realize just how crucial having discernment and renouncing self-doubt would be.

❧❧❧

By December 2008, Tanner's business ventures had expanded tremendously. He sat me down one night and showed me a few of his recent contracts. "I know these numbers are big and might be hard to wrap your head around, Sydney, but they're legit," he said.

I sucked in my breath as I stared at the numbers before me. Billions. Not millions of dollars, but billions. More money than most people in the world will ever lay eyes on. It shocked me.

"That's ... crazy," I stammered.

"Yup, crazy but true. This thing is like a wildfire," Tanner agreed.

I kept the numbers to myself and didn't share the success with our friends and family. As far as anyone knew, we were just an adventurous newlywed couple living in Manhattan, pursuing our dreams.

In 2009, I was asked to be on a leadership team of 10 women at the church Tanner and I attended in the city. One day, during a team-building event, the inspirational leader stopped and told me that God had a word for me.

"Promotion is the word God is giving me," she said boldly in front of the entire team of women. "You have been in a season where you've been held back, and you will now move forward."

Immediately following this, another leader at the meeting spoke up: "God gave me a vision of you. I saw a bride coming down an aisle, veiled and holding a candle high in the air. As she approached the end of the aisle, her veil came off. I believe God is saying that while things have seemed uncertain, you've stayed grounded and faithful to him, holding your head high, even when you've been unsure of what is ahead. You are coming to the end of this journey, and light will shine in the darkness as God opens new doors and a new season is unveiled in your life."

Whoa. God continued to confirm that he was going to open doors for me. I had to trust that though this was a time to take a step back, things wouldn't always be this way. That day the meeting ended as the team of 10 women stopped and prayed for me, encouraging me to trust in the Lord. I was awed and grateful for their discernment and care.

A few weeks later, the first of many bombs dropped onto my marriage.

Running Shoes

❧❧❧❧

While going through my e-mails one morning, I stopped at one in particular. It was from a good friend I had grown up with who had moved to New York City to pursue her career. She had partnered with Tanner's business against my wishes; I had told him from the start that I preferred that he not work with friends or family, lest things get messy.

And things had gotten messy.

"I have good reason to believe that your husband is practicing unethical business," the friend began. She went on to list several red flags she had seen over the past few months. "I'm sorry, but I am ending all involvement with Tanner's company."

I sank into my chair, my heart racing as I re-read the e-mail. Could the things she told me be true? As a friend of hers for years, I had no reason to doubt the legitimacy of her words; yet, they were huge, life changing even. I felt like I'd been slugged in the chest with a baseball bat. Now what should I do? Confront Tanner? Let it go and pretend I didn't care?

Panicked and confused, I called up a close family friend and business partner of Tanner's. I considered him a highly respectable person, both spiritually and ethically. He was aware of the huge amounts of money being exchanged, and I trusted him to tell me what move to make next. "What do you make of all this?" I asked him after I'd showed him the e-mail.

Resound

He took a deep breath. "You need to trust your husband, and don't be critical."

It wasn't the answer I thought he would give; I'd half expected him to fly out of his seat and confirm the seriousness of it. But instead, he encouraged me to hold tight and trust that my husband knew what he was doing. I still felt I had to say something to Tanner.

When I sat Tanner down and showed him the e-mail, he hardly seemed fazed. "Look, I gotta tell you something, Sydney. This friend of yours, she's not quite right. In fact, I'd call her a bit crazy. This whole e-mail is nonsense. You have to believe me; her intentions really aren't good. It's definitely for the best that she's no longer working with us, because I just don't trust her."

I gasped. Something in my gut didn't agree, but I played along, anyway. "Well, she always seemed solid and ethical to me, but I trust you," I said, trying to heed the words of my family friend.

The loneliness ate away at me again. I didn't feel I could call my family or friends back home and confide in them, so instead I called up the couple we'd become close with in New York. I quickly met up with them, took a deep breath and shared my newfound information. During this conversation they revealed they had lent Tanner large sums of money. I was shocked.

"I have to tell you, Tanner told us he would pay us back, but we haven't seen a dime in six months," the husband told me, shaking his head.

My blood started to boil. Here sat a couple who had

accepted us like family and had been nothing but loyal, kind and generous toward us since we moved to Manhattan. I now had to face the fact that Tanner had been deceiving them as well, and it was almost too much for me to bear. "Pray for me. I'm going to try to get to the bottom of this," I said with a long sigh.

I confronted Tanner again. "Tell me what's really going on," I demanded.

"Look, it's complicated, okay? We only get paid when someone else's contract closes, and those sort of things don't always work out so neatly," he explained huffily. "You really need to just let this go and trust me, Sydney."

I wanted to, oh, how I wanted to. I wanted to believe in my husband, wanted to believe he was still the great man of God I had married. Things had seemed so perfect, almost too perfect. I'd only wanted what every other girl wants: a marriage filled with happiness. And up until this point, I'd really believed I had it. Now what was I to do?

Desperate, I called my family and confided in them at last. "I really don't know what to do," I said. "I want to trust my husband, but things just aren't adding up, and he's only growing more distant."

"I wish we were closer," my mom said sadly. Even thousands of miles away, I could tell her heart was heavy for me. "Can you arrange to meet with your close friends and your pastor there and try to make some headway?"

I asked Tanner if he felt comfortable having a meeting with our friends and pastor. To my surprise, he agreed. A few days later, we sat across from these people, going back and forth for hours in what I can only describe as the most horribly intense day of my life. I cried, pleading with him to be honest with me. In turn, he blamed our troubles on me.

"Our marriage isn't doing very well, that's all," he explained. "You're making things really difficult for me, Sydney."

I was floored that he would turn the tables on me at my desperate hour. "What do you expect me to do? You won't tell me anything!" I lashed back.

"You really threw me under the bus in there," Tanner hissed when the exhausting session was over. "Thanks a lot."

After cooling off, however, Tanner agreed to go to counseling with me. "I love you, and I want to make things right between us again," he assured me. "Please let me do that, okay?" In his eyes, I saw a glimpse of the wonderful man I had married.

I nodded through my tears. "I will try." For the next few months, I prayed over my marriage like I never had before. I cried out to God, asking him to help my husband be a man of character, a man who still wanted to serve and love him. I felt God near to me, his peace only a heartfelt prayer away. I had to hang on and choose to believe that God would restore our marriage and make things right again.

The year 2009 was a pivotal year for the business. Tanner became busier than ever, flying off to various places around the globe last minute, always telling me he had to duck out for a business lunch or dinner. While he continued to insist that they were on the brink of something big, my heart remained cautious. I began poking around our house and discovered a few suspicious things.

"What's this new bottle of cologne doing in your drawer?" I asked one evening as I cleaned our bathroom. I held up a very expensive name-brand bottle of cologne; being a fashion lover myself, I knew the brand had only released the cologne a few days ago.

"Oh, that. My mom picked it up for me at TJ Maxx," he replied casually.

A few days later, I found a few packages of new boxer briefs in his drawer. I thought this strange, since he usually just asked me to buy him those if he needed them. I also found a brand-new pair of shoes I'd never seen before; he claimed someone else bought them and passed them on to him. Not long after that, I discovered a new suit hanging in the back of his closet.

"Where did this come from?" I demanded, tossing the suit onto the bed.

"That's just an old suit I've had forever," he explained.

My fingers trembled as I hung the suit back in the closet. "It looks brand new to me," I replied, trying to keep a steady voice. *Lies, lies, I knew they were all lies.* Yet demanding the truth didn't seem to get me anywhere. The only answer Tanner had was to back off and trust him.

I needed more proof that something was seriously wrong, but where could I turn next?

Resound

ぷぷぷ

In June 2009, Tanner's parents came to visit. One night when they were out, he called to tell me he'd lost his wedding ring. "I'm so sorry, babe. It just fell off in the cab … I couldn't believe it. I looked down, and it was just gone."

At this point, that ring didn't seem to mean much, anyway. It signified trust, love and honor, all qualities that had been lost over the past few months. "Well, are you going to get a new one?" I asked flatly.

"Of course." But weeks went by, and he didn't seem eager to replace the ring. This saddened me but did not surprise me.

One evening, Tanner told me he was going to help some friends move. "I'll be back early this evening," he promised. He came home around dinnertime and insisted he needed to go back again. I thought this was strange, but I let him go without question.

It was nearly 2 a.m. when Tanner finally walked through the door. I lay in bed, staring out at the Hudson, a horrid feeling in my stomach. I had fallen in love with this condo for the view; looking out at the water made me feel peaceful, gave me hope. But tonight, I felt nothing but anger and disappointment.

"Where were you?" I asked, too weary to put up a fight.

"Oh, Crate and Barrel got backed up with their deliveries, and it just took forever," he said, slipping out of his clothes. He climbed into bed and planted a kiss on my cheek. I felt sick; there was a time when I wanted nothing more than to kiss my husband until we were breathless, but right now, I wished he were far, far away.

The red flags continued to pop up. Next came a credit card bill in the mail. As I scanned it, my heart sank. The expenses listed on the bill were supposedly for a business trip to Europe, but the expenses seemed extravagant; I had a hard time believing they were all business related. As I set the bill back on the desk, I found it difficult to breathe. My fairytale life was beginning to feel a lot more like a horror movie.

My life was spinning wildly out of control.

That same day a good friend of mine came to stay with us for the week and brought along her daughter. I focused on showing them the sights of the city and tried to put things out of my mind. They left on a Saturday morning; on Sunday, I sat down to check my e-mail and was surprised to see one pop up from my friend and Tanner's former business partner.

"Sydney, I am deeply concerned for you," she wrote. "I have had no other choice but to take legal action against your husband. I hope that you will soon find the answers you need."

Shaking, I went to Tanner and confronted him once again. "What are you going to tell me about all these accusations?" I asked, trying to reign in my anger.

Tanner set down his laptop and glared at me. "Look, this girl is crazy. But since she won't seem to go away, I think we should appease her and try to meet with her. Just the three of us, no attorneys involved. Get her off our case once and for all."

Our case? Was this really *our* case? Nothing made sense anymore. After the first e-mail, Tanner had insisted I have no further contact with our friend due to legal reasons; now he was telling me to call her to meet! Once again, I felt myself at a loss. At last, I responded to her, saying we wanted to meet, but I didn't hear a word back.

It was just one more rung in the ladder of hurt. How could I ever find out what was going on?

෩෩෩෩

Tanner grew more and more distant and busier and busier. I threw myself into volunteer activities for several nonprofits in the city and tried to keep my focus on God. He was the one thing that remained unchanging in my life, the only thing I could count on anymore. Despite the loss, the loneliness and the lies, I clung to what I knew to be true: God's unfaltering love for me.

In October, I sat in church one Sunday evening, my heart wracked with confusion and sadness. The Lord suddenly spoke to me through the pastor's message from a passage in Ezekiel 37: *Life to dead bones.* He used an analogy of a pot of soup: If you don't stir a pot of soup, all the ingredients sink to the bottom. He likened this to our God-given gifts. If we don't use them, they go dormant. I felt like the pastor was speaking directly to me. "There are gifted people here, Sydney, but all of your gifts have sunk to the bottom of the pot of soup."

This message spoke to my heart in a powerful way, and I felt God was confirming that he was going to stir me in this coming season. That those "gifts" that had been dormant would soon become active in my life again. I took great hope in this; it seemed to go along with the other words of confirmation the Lord had given me. This was a difficult season of unknowns, but God wasn't finished with me yet. I had to keep holding on.

Later during the service, the worship team sang the lyrics "we will live and not die." My heart sang for joy for the first time in a long while. I had been dead for months, my spirit devoid of joy, but God promised to bring me back to life and give me hope again.

The next day, I met with the pastor's wife. She encouraged me to step out in different avenues in my life and believe in miracles. I had been praying all year for miracles, and her word confirmed this even more in my heart.

I had a feeling my story was about to take a huge turn.

৵৵৵

On a Wednesday night, I sat in front of a mirror, carefully applying makeup, choosing my best jewelry and styling my hair. I slipped into my best cocktail dress and completed the outfit with my favorite pair of stilettos. I had been looking forward to this big night for weeks;

Resound

Tanner and I had been invited to a posh art gala in the city. It would be a great chance to network, enjoy a night on the town and, of course, see some great art. Despite our privately rocky marriage, I secretly hoped tonight would be magical, that we would be able to put the difficulties of the past months behind us for one evening and enjoy ourselves.

"I'm not sure I want to go," Tanner said at the last minute, coming out of the bathroom in his suit. He looked more handsome than ever, and I found myself desperately wanting to believe the man beneath the buttoned-up shirt and tie still loved me till death do us part.

"What do you mean? You love this kind of stuff!" I laughed at the absurdity.

"Yeah, well, I dunno." He tugged at his tie. "I guess we can go."

I was surprised by his sudden lack of enthusiasm but brushed it off as we headed out the door.

The art gala was held at a beautiful loft in Lower Manhattan; the minute we stepped off the elevator, I was in awe. I took in the sea of shiny cocktail dresses, the dapper men in their suits, the mouth-watering hors d'oeuvres. I was just about to help myself to a drink when I looked back and saw that Tanner had disappeared. I searched the entire room for him but to no avail. At last, I slipped out and found him getting ready to slip into the descending elevator.

"What are you doing?" I asked, confused.

"Not feeling good," he muttered.

Running Shoes

He explained that he wasn't much for these parties and just wanted to be alone with me. I reluctantly agreed to go with him. Just as we stepped off the elevator, the host of the event stepped on, looking surprised to see us leaving. "Going so soon? The party just started!" he hollered, slapping Tanner playfully on the back.

Tanner nodded toward me as though to say, "It's her, not me." Furious, I dug my heels into the ground and tried to keep a casual smile on my face.

"What was that all about?" I asked when we were in the cab. "You made me look like a jerk!"

Tanner slipped his hand over mine. "Babe, I just wanted it to be the two of us tonight. You look so beautiful, and I was really hoping to just take you to a nice restaurant so we could have some peace and quiet." He kissed me softly. "Have I told you lately how much I love you?"

I tried to give into his flattery and let myself believe he was sincere. We spent the night at an intimate restaurant, where he wined and dined me and told me he was so happy I was his wife. To any casual observer, we probably looked like two lovebirds out on the town. Little did they know the pain that lie between us, so thick it would take a miracle to break through.

The following night, Tanner emerged from the bathroom wearing jeans and a blazer. "I'm off to a business meeting, as usual," he called out.

I glanced up. "Wearing that?" Business meetings usually involved suits and ties in New York City.

Resound

"Yeah, it's just casual tonight."

As he left, I stared after him, a horrid feeling sinking into my bones. All the red flags suddenly culminated in that moment as I realized once and for all that something was terribly, terribly wrong.

I happened to be doing my Bible study that evening on the book of Esther. The study discussed facing one's biggest fears. I realized I had been paralyzed with fear all this time; angst overtook me until I could no longer finish my lesson. I set the book down and instead began to furiously clean the house from top to bottom.

Tanner texted later that night to say he'd be home by 10. When 11:15 rolled around, I tried calling him incessantly, but he didn't answer. I tried again until he finally picked up his phone. "Sorry, got stuck in the subway," he said quickly.

The subway? Tanner hated the subway; he always took a cab. I furiously hung up the phone; the minute he got home, I completely fell apart. "I don't know what's going on, but you have to tell me … right now!" I cried.

"I don't know if I love you anymore," Tanner said sadly, sinking onto our bed.

I grabbed his phone and scanned his texts, catching a couple interactions between him and other women. "What's this all about? Is there another woman?!" I cried.

"I've entertained thoughts of other women," Tanner said slowly.

෯෯෯

Running Shoes

My heart convulsed with fear. I called my parents and spilled everything with Tanner sitting right there. I handed him the phone when I was done, as he agreed to talk to my parents.

"It's all true," he confirmed. "Sydney really needs a break. I think she should go back to Portland for a while."

Tanner bought me a plane ticket that evening, and by the next afternoon, I found myself at JFK heading back to Portland. Having cried myself to sleep, I was physically and emotionally exhausted when the plane landed. My parents greeted me with open arms. They shared that they had been heavily burdened for me for the past several months and had been praying faithfully; God had prepared them for the heartbreaking phone call.

A close group of girlfriends in Portland were just getting ready to embark on an annual girls' weekend. I joined them last minute and confided in them on our trip. While our annual trips in the past had included lots of laughs, walks on the beach and strolls through the beach town, this weekend held a more somber tone as they prayed over me and my marriage. I was grateful God had orchestrated things so that I could attend this getaway and be encouraged by my dear friends.

I had been training for the New York City Marathon for months; it was something I'd set my heart on accomplishing, and I'd looked forward to it as an outlet for my adrenaline and my spirit. Determined not to let my painful circumstances deter me from the big day, I flew back to New York a week later, along with my father, brother and a best friend. On November 1, 2009, I completed my first marathon, running alongside my brother. It felt exhilarating to cross that finish line, knowing I'd accomplished such a feat. I felt victorious despite my brokenness inside.

The next day they helped me pack up my clothes, and I returned to Portland, where I began counseling and tried to get to the bottom of Tanner's many lies. "Lord, please shine light onto the darkness," I prayed over and over. I started studying bank records, phone bills, e-mails and social networking sites and slowly, piece by piece, discovered the painful, horrible truth.

My husband had been living a double life — in more ways than one.

Through various phone calls and investigations, I learned that not only had Tanner been involved in unethical business practices and business ventures I was completely unaware of, but he had also been involved with other women. Several other women. Learning about the other women was infinitely more painful than the rest of the events. I could hardly wrap my head around the fact that he had been with me one hour and another woman the next. My mind wandered to that moment he'd run out of the much-anticipated art gala; perhaps spotting one of these other women explained that strange behavior.

Suddenly, nothing, from the moment we met in that van in San Diego to the last moments we'd spent together in New York City, felt true. Who was this man I had married and fallen in love with?

Running Shoes

✿✿✿

Tanner's lies escalated during our separation. At first, when we spoke on the phone, I went along with them, hoping I could garner some new information.

"The government in Haiti is flying me out there to help them with their economic plan after the earthquake," he told me one morning.

"No one is flying in there right now," I protested.

"Oh, we're taking a private jet to an aircraft carrier that will then ship us into port," he said quickly.

He also claimed he had flown out to meet with Gaddafi, the president of Libya. He also declared he was working with certain large businesses in Manhattan, yet when I investigated the companies further, they'd never heard of him before.

They were lies, all lies, and I knew it, yet I played along until I had the cold hard facts in my hands.

One day, a friend introduced me to the word "sociopath."

I read up on it and got the chills, as I realized that the definition fit Tanner almost to a tee. Sociopaths are infamous for being charismatic, full of superficial charm, masters of manipulation, pathological liars, unfaithful to their spouses and without remorse. They often talk of grandiose ideas and making lots of money, but in reality they are con-artists. For the first time, I was confronted with the horrible fact that Tanner had something seriously mentally wrong with him.

Resound

The parallel characteristics of a sociopath to the man I had married were striking.

Heartbroken, I recounted every detail of our marriage. I had fallen in love with Tanner because of his passion for me, the Lord and for life. Initially, I had even considered him a bit too conservative for me, feeling guilty to read one of my favorite style or gossip magazines around him.

How could a man who had boldly preached, led worship in church and pointed young people to a relationship with God be the same man who now squandered money on Wall Street and had multiple affairs?

∽∽∽

In June 2010, Tanner and I were officially divorced. He never offered an apology, nor did he return any of my personal belongings or provide a sense of closure, but instead continued to live a lavish life of lies in New York City. At times, I got angry, wishing justice to be served, but I reminded myself that God is the ultimate avenger and through him truth will ultimately be known. Meanwhile, I began my healing journey toward restoration, seeking the Lord for the next step of my life.

Moving back to Portland was not only painful, but humbling as well. I had fallen in love with New York City and grieved the loss of the people and places that had become home. Now divorced and living with my parents, I was forced to completely start over without a dollar to my name. There were days I woke up and wondered, *How can this possibly be my life?*

But in the stillness and the sadness, God spoke to me, reminding me of his steadfast love and giving me hope. I read the Bible verse, Isaiah 42:16: "I will lead the blind along ways they have not known, along unfamiliar paths. I will guide them; I will turn the darkness into light before them and make the rough places smooth. These are the things I will do; I will not forsake them."

He had indeed answered my prayers, turning darkness into light, proving through his faithfulness that he had not forsaken me in my loneliness and despair.

❧❧❧

My father introduced me to Pastor Luke and Alissa Reid of the newly formed Resound Church in Portland, Oregon. "I think you will really like this place."

Eager for a fresh start, I attended a service and fell in love with the gracious people there. They welcomed me with open arms, taking a broken girl in with such love that I knew at once this would be my home church for the time God had me in Portland.

Since I've shared my story with others, several women have come forward and told me similar stories about their destructive marriages or broken-hearted journeys. I've been able to cry with them and encourage them to hold onto the only hope we can count on, the hope in Jesus Christ. I look back on the words of those who spoke over me: "God will open doors for you." The doors he's opened are not the doors I thought I'd walk through, but I can now see glimpses of the good plan he has for my life. I believe that slowly, those "gifts" on the bottom of the pot will find their way to the top, and God will use me to encourage and inspire others with a message of his sustaining power and hope.

In November 2010, I flew back to New York City and ran the New York City Marathon as my victory race, a celebration for surviving the first year of my radical and unexpected life change. As my running shoes hit the pavement and the crowd cheered me on, a fresh wave of adrenaline overtook me, along with something more important: joy. The moment I crossed the finish line, I felt like maybe I could conquer the world. It was a true moment of victory and healing in my heart.

My journey is far from over, but I do know this: Despite our circumstances, God is faithful. If we keep our eyes on him, we will not lose hope. Life may look bleak, but in those dark moments, we must always fight for light over darkness, healing over pain, dancing over mourning.

As we slip on our running shoes and sprint to the finish line, we can find him there, waiting with open arms, celebrating our victory.

The Unexpected Gift
The Story of Cathryn
Written by Karen Koczwara

Please, please let it be "no."

I am sitting in a bathroom stall inside Target, holding what may be the most significant purchase of my life. A tiny white plastic stick determines my future; a "no" means I can take a deep breath of relief, a "yes" means things will never be the same.

How did I get here? Here is not just the Target bathroom stall with the white plastic stick. Here is this ache in my heart that won't go away, these decisions that haunt me day and night, a life that's unraveled into a mess. Here is certainly not where I thought I would be a year ago.

Slowly, I open my eyes, and there on the stick, clear as can be, is a "yes." Three letters, glaring at me, undeniable. My heart quickens. My worst fear has become a reality; there is a baby inside of me.

My hands shake as I stuff the stick back in the bag and walk out of the stall. Shoppers brush by me, carts in hand, hurried and unaware that my life has just changed in that bathroom stall. I weave in between them and push through the doors into the bright sunlight. Somehow, my two feet propel me to my car, and somehow, I start the engine.

Pregnant. Alone. Afraid. How did I get *here?*

Resound

᠅᠅᠅

From the outside looking in, my childhood seemed idyllic. I was born in 1985 to two loving parents in Portland, Oregon. My father was a Bible school graduate, and both my parents were heavily involved in church. My brother Jared arrived exactly three years after I came along; we were inseparable. Just after his birth, my father left his roofing business, Kings Roofing Service, and moved our family to Whidbey Island, Washington, to pursue becoming a police officer. Just as my father earned his officer badge, the rest of our lives slowly unraveled.

When I was 6 years old, my mother came to Jared and me, her usually bright eyes lifeless and sad. "Kids, Mommy is going to move you back to Portland," she said, her voice cracking. "Daddy is going to stay here for a while."

"Because he's a police officer now?" I asked, confused.

"Yes," she said with a sigh.

And just as quickly as we'd come, we were gone. My mother took Jared and me back to Portland, where we settled into a tiny house with a giant backyard. The yard promised tree houses and forts and late summer nights running through the sprinklers, but instead, it felt empty and lonely without my father around.

Jared's and my birthday rolled around in March, and I waited eagerly for my father to arrive. Surely, he would not forget our birthdays! But when dinner came and went and he still had not come, I sat on the couch and burst into tears.

The Unexpected Gift

"Daddy doesn't love me anymore," I sobbed.

"Oh, yes, he does, honey." My mother left the room and returned with two tiny cupcakes, one for Jared and me. "Now, let's make this a happy birthday, shall we?" She lit the candles and began to sing, a feeble attempt to cheer us up.

I slowly bit into the cupcake, but my appetite was gone. "Daddy doesn't love me," I repeated, wiping my tears away.

My mother reached for the phone. A few moments later, she handed it to me.

"Happy birthday, sweetie!" It was my father's voice on the line.

"Thanks," I mumbled, the cupcake sticking in my throat. "When you coming home?"

"I don't know just yet, but I do know this. I love you very much. I always have, and I always will," he replied.

He sounded so far away. I tried to believe him, but at 6 years old, I just wanted him here, blowing out the candles next to me on the couch.

Nearly 10 months after we'd moved back, my father returned. He got a job as a police officer and moved us into a beautiful white stucco house on a cul-de-sac. Not long after, my mother announced that a new baby was on the way. I was thrilled to have my father back and elated to be a big sister again. Life, it seemed, had returned to normal.

My mother gave birth to another boy; they named him Chad. I was sure we could all get along just fine in the big

white stucco house. But then the fighting began —
squabbles that escalated into terrifying screaming matches
while my brothers and I hovered in the other room. One
evening, I heard my mother yelling at my father in the
kitchen.

"This can't keep going on! I thought you were done
with this!" my mother cried shrilly.

I peeked around the corner and was horrified to see
my mother grab a large knife from the counter. She hurled
it at my father; he caught it just before it pierced his chest.
Trembling, I hid behind the couch with my brothers,
trying to comfort them as the screaming continued.

"Why are Mommy and Daddy yelling again?"Jared
whimpered.

"They're just having a little fight," I replied, my voice
faltering as I tried to keep strong.

It was a terrible year for me. I hated my parents
fighting, hated my third grade teacher with her bright red
lipstick and hated the red itchy patches that began to pop
up all over my skin. My mother took me to the doctor
when the patches spread. *Psoriasis,* he said. I wore
turtlenecks despite the hot temperatures to cover up the
embarrassment. But beneath my skin, a deeper pain
brewed.

My father returned to his roofing business and
continued to succeed. We put a swimming pool and a
pond in the backyard, but this did little to ease the fighting
at home. One night, I went to a friend's for a sleepover.
Just as we were settling into our sleeping bags, my mother

came to the door and told me we needed to leave. Her entire face was streaked with mascara; I was terrified.

"What's wrong, Mom?" I asked, panicked, as we sped away.

"Your father and I are getting a divorce," she blurted. "Your father has done some very bad things."

Very bad things? Divorce? But divorce was for people who didn't believe in God! My family went to church every Sunday. My parents were respected leaders, Bible scholars! We'd even taken a troubled woman into our home for a time. People with big houses and swimming pools who went to church every Sunday weren't supposed to get divorced.

My mother told me the story through her tears. A drunk woman had shown up on our porch that night. She told my mother she had been seeing my father for the past two years.

She had finally given him an ultimatum: your family or me. Angry when he would not choose, she drove to our house with my father and spilled everything while my father panicked and circled the neighborhood in the car. My mother freaked out and called the police.

I was shocked. "Did Dad kiss this other lady?" I asked in horror. My father was a good man; I couldn't picture him in the arms of another woman.

"Yes, honey," my mother said quietly.

That night, I fell to the ground weeping. "Why, God? Why is all this happening? I love my dad. How could he do this to us?" I cried.

Resound

As my tears soaked the carpet, I suddenly felt goose bumps prickle my flesh. The presence of God overcame me, and I heard him whisper to me, "It's okay, my daughter. Everything is going to be okay."

More tears came in a flood as I felt God, very near and real to me in the stillness of the night. I had spent my whole life sitting in church, hearing all the Bible stories, praying the prayers. But until now, I hadn't felt God's presence like this. My soul sang for joy as I realized that, despite my pain and confusion, I was not alone.

My father moved out shortly after, leaving us behind in our house to crumble. I grew angry, trying to sort out the lies from the truth. Not long ago, my father had taken me to get my ears pierced. Now, suddenly, this felt like a lie. All those times he'd said he loved me, taken me in his arms or up on his knee — those, too, were false. If my father had been living a lie for two years, what on earth was real?

The church quickly got wind of my father's despicable actions and excommunicated him. I spent the next few weeks reeling from shock, trying to figure out where we'd all gone wrong. One morning, as I brushed my teeth, I noticed that one side of my face looked strange. I also couldn't taste the toothpaste in half my mouth. Panicked, I ran to my mother's room, where she now spent her days lying on the bed sobbing.

"Something's wrong with me!" I cried.

A trip to the doctor revealed a strange condition: Bell's Palsy. "This is brought on by traumatic events or stress,"

The Unexpected Gift

the doctor explained. "There isn't much we can do; it will go away on its own."

This wasn't much comfort for a girl just about to enter junior high. As though things weren't bad enough at home, I now had to deal with a half-paralyzed face! My brothers tried to make me laugh, thinking it funny to see me try to smile. Nothing felt very amusing about my situation, however. My life was truly falling apart.

Unable to afford our big beautiful house, my mother moved my brothers and me into a small townhome. Having only known life as a stay-at-home mom, my mother had no degree and was forced to draw upon welfare. We had to get rid of our beloved black lab, Shadow. My brothers and I sobbed as a man came to pick him up and take him away one afternoon. Overnight, we had gone from riches to rags, having lost everything dear in our lives.

Just when it seemed things couldn't unravel any further, they did. My father became addicted to meth; his mistress had been a meth addict, and he soon took after her ways. Once a respected police officer, my father now found himself in jail for dealing drugs and for theft. The man who had once bounced me on his knee and taken me to church was now unrecognizable.

As I neared high school, I became determined to be nothing like my father. I threw myself into church and youth ministry, memorizing the entire book of James in the Bible in eighth grade. I stayed far away from boys, convinced that they were a waste of time. I became the quintessential good girl and took great pride in my dedication to church. Meanwhile, God completely healed my face from the Bell's Palsy, and I thanked him for answering my prayers.

Our home was broken, but I refused to let my spirit be, too. I stuffed my pain away for the time being and spent all my free time at youth group. I visited my father in jail a few times, disgusted by the man he had become. I wondered if he ever thought about the white stucco house with the swimming pool and wished he hadn't made so many wrong turns.

After high school, I started Bible college, still determined to be the best Christian girl I could be. I ignored the boys and threw myself into my studies, still hopeful that my life might turn out different than my father's. I lived on campus for the first year and then moved in with my best friend Jenny and her parents, John and Karen. Meanwhile, I tucked away the pain that gnawed at my soul; if I kept busy, perhaps it wouldn't find me.

"My ex-girlfriend's dad is crazy. He's been following me, trying to kill me," my father told me one day when I visited. "I've got to get out of this city." He had gone to rehab and was supposed to be sorting out his life, but things were only growing more complicated.

I didn't know whether or not to believe him. So far, my entire childhood felt like a bundle of lies; how could I begin to sort out the truth now? But soon enough, we all realized my father was telling the truth. He had become involved in dangerous pursuits and now had detectives on his tail. Maybe he did need to get out of town.

"Your aunt and uncle say there's work down in San Diego," my father said. They were youth pastors at a church there. "Maybe a little sun wouldn't hurt, eh?"

He got a construction job in San Diego and made the big move down south. After a year, my aunt and uncle took a position as youth pastors in Las Vegas, and my father followed them. Soon after, my brother Chad, who had been partying heavily and hanging out with a bad crowd of kids, joined my father in Las Vegas. I had graduated Bible college and decided to visit during Thanksgiving week.

Though my relationship with my father was still strained, I enjoyed the week I spent in Las Vegas. As my visit came to an end, I began praying about moving there for good. Perhaps a change of scenery would be the first step toward healing in our family.

As I prayed, I asked the Lord for 10 specific things, hoping to receive confirmation on all of them before I flew back to Oregon. On Sunday morning, the day before I was to leave, I visited the church where my uncle was a youth pastor; a woman was speaking on physical healing. As she neared the end of her message, she abruptly asked the whole back row to stand up. Slowly, I stood to my feet and felt her eyes directly on me.

"Second Corinthians 1:20: 'For no matter how many promises God has made they are all yes in Christ and so through him the amen is spoken today by the glory of God'," she began.

She then held up 10 fingers, looked at me and said, "Yes, yes, yes …" 10 times! I felt my heart race. This message was specifically for me!

"Okay, Lord, I guess you want me in Vegas," I whispered, my heart filling with peace.

I returned to Portland and went back to work as the scheduling manager for a large company. I confided in a few co-workers that I felt God calling me to Vegas, and word soon got back to my boss.

"Cathryn, we're making a real investment by having you here," he told me. "You need to give us a year commitment if you are planning to stay with us."

"I … I can't do that," I replied quietly.

"Well, then, it looks like we will need to find someone else for the job," he replied. "You'll receive a month's severance pay. Best of luck to you."

I collected my severance check and reminded myself that this was all part of God's plan. On January 1, 2007, I packed up the rest of my things and moved to Vegas. It was New Year's Day, the perfect time for a fresh start, a new chapter in my life. I had no idea what the future held, but since God had confirmed the move, I had to believe he had a plan.

Two weeks after my move, I landed a job as a staff assistant to one of the pastors at the church I had attended. During one of my first days on the job, I met Jeremy, an intern at the church who oversaw the junior

The Unexpected Gift

high ministry. We began dating six months later; he was my very first boyfriend.

Six months into our relationship, Jeremy asked me to marry him and I accepted. As we planned our wedding, however, those closest to me pulled me aside to share their concern. "Are you sure this is your husband, Cathryn?" my father asked.

"Yes, of course," I replied hastily. I was still resentful of my father and determined to prove to him that I could have a successful marriage despite his failures.

My pastor came to me next. "I'm afraid that you are too strong for Jeremy," he said gently. "I don't think he's spiritually strong enough to be married to you."

"Thanks for your advice, but I plan to go through with the wedding," I replied. Since I had never dated before, I really had no idea what love was; I had no one to compare Jeremy to. I figured that if God had brought him into my life, he must be the one for me. Little did I know what a difficult road I was about to walk down.

My father had been dating a beautiful woman and planned to marry her. I asked him to please respect me by not marrying her until after my wedding. He agreed to and also agreed to pay for the flowers for my ceremony. As my big day approached, a gnawing anxiety grew in my heart. I tried to ignore it as I tried my dress on one last time, but it settled deep inside of me and stayed.

On the night of the dress rehearsal, I found out my father had asked his girlfriend to marry him. Horrified, I pulled my father aside. "I thought you promised not to propose to her until after our wedding!" I hissed. "And where are the flowers?"

"I'm really sorry, but …" His face flamed like a kid caught reaching in the cookie jar.

"You blew the flower money on a ring?!" I was raising my voice and didn't even care. How could he do such a thing? We had just climbed the first rung on the ladder of our new relationship, and now we were back on the ground. I was furious that he had gone against his word and that I now had no flowers for my big day.

Most girls wake up on their wedding day filled with the usual flutters of excitement in their stomach, but the flutters in my chest felt more like dread and apprehension than bubbly joy.

"If my fiancée can't sit in the front with me at the ceremony, I'm going to sit in the back," my father announced shortly before the wedding ceremony.

Is this Try to Ruin Your Daughter's Wedding Day? I wondered angrily as he left the room. My blood boiled. "God, when are you going to change him?" I cried out.

I was determined not to let anyone ruin my special day, but when my father walked me down the aisle, anger brewed inside; it was difficult to find joy in the moment. When my father stood up to give a speech, I stood there gritting my teeth and tuning out his words.

As the pastor pronounced us man and wife that hot June afternoon, the lump in my chest returned. And that night, supposedly the most glorious night in a woman's life, I cried myself to sleep. "This is not how it is supposed to be," my heart whispered. "What if everyone was right? What if we're not meant to be together?"

The next day, my mother called and dropped a bombshell of her own.

"I know this may come as a shock to you, but I've gotten remarried," she announced.

I was speechless. My mother had been dating a guy for about a year, but they weren't even engaged, and now she was telling me she was married a day after my own wedding! It was too much to handle at once. I hung up the phone, furious and reeling with shock. I'd been married fewer than 24 hours, and already things were beginning to feel disastrous.

Jeremy and I fell into a day-to-day rhythm, going about our busy lives as newlyweds. I landed a new job at a communications company and enjoyed the fast-paced work. We both became involved as youth pastors at the church and loved reaching out to the next generation. For the first few months, things were okay. I didn't feel that passion so many people talked about when they married the love of their life, but I wasn't miserable, either. *Maybe this is just the way it's supposed to be,* I thought sadly.

Christmas rolled around, and my company threw a big holiday party at the Palms Club. Despite living in Vegas for some time now, I had spent little time in the casinos and was completely naive to the party scene. Our company set us up with a VIP room, complete with all the alcohol we could consume. After dinner, Jeremy leaned over and hollered over the noise, "I have to work early in the morning, so I think I'm gonna head home. Why don't you stay here and get drunk?"

"Excuse me?" I retorted.

"Yeah, just stay here and get drunk." He kissed my head and disappeared, leaving me alone to figure out a way to get home. And get drunk.

I had never gotten drunk in my life and was shocked that my own husband would suggest I do such a thing. While my peers had partied their way through high school and college, I had holed up in my room, studying scripture and praying. While my family had unraveled at the seams, I had dug my heels in the ground and tried to remain faithful to God. But where had it gotten me, really? Here, in a loveless marriage, confused and alone? Maybe Jeremy's idea wasn't so bad after all.

"Hey, I need a drink!" I stood up and marched to the bar.

"Whoa, get the girl a drink!" one of my co-workers hollered. "Look, everyone, Cathryn's drinkin' tonight!"

Suddenly, people lined up right and left to buy me drinks. I threw all caution to the wind and downed them like they were water, one after another, tossing out a piece of my soul with each swig. Before long, I was drunk. I ran around the room, waving my arms and laughing. "Look at me, everyone! I'm a Christian, and I'm getting drunk!"

Everyone laughed back, and in that moment, something shifted in my world. The room spun around me, the bright lights blurred as the music blared and I felt … alive. Free. Happy, even.

The Unexpected Gift

Maybe all those years I'd had my nose in the Bible I'd really been missing out!

A co-worker and his wife gave me a ride home that night. The next morning, I awoke with a hangover. "So, you did it, huh? You really got drunk!" My husband laughed as I rubbed my bleary eyes.

"You think it's funny?" I asked, incredulous.

"Well, yeah, don't you?" He laughed again as he headed off to work.

Anger and insecurity simultaneously overcame me as I replayed the events of the night and my husband's response to my behavior. My pastor's words echoed in my head, haunting me in the moment: "He's not a spiritual leader." Was it really true? Just a few weeks ago, I'd tried to get Jeremy to pray with me before bed. It was what Christian couples did together, after all. But he had been too absorbed in his video games to want to sit down in prayer. Defeated, I'd left the room and didn't ask him again.

A cute security guard at the mall where I worked as a manager at a kiosk began flirting with me. I enjoyed his attention and flirted back. One day on my way to work, I casually slid my wedding ring off and slipped it in my purse. When he asked for my phone number one evening, I blurted out my digits.

That night, as I made Jeremy dinner and settled onto the couch with him to watch a movie, the security guard, Joe, texted me. Sitting just inches from my husband, I texted him back. We exchanged several flirtatious texts;

my heart raced with excitement and horror at how easy it was. *What are you doing, Cathryn?* a little voice inside cried out. *This isn't who you are.* But the attention felt good, and I didn't want to give it up. Especially when things were so strained at home.

"Hey, you up for a movie?" Joe asked one evening as we got off work. "A bunch of us are going."

It's harmless, I told myself. *Just a few friends catching a flick; what could possibly happen?* I called Jeremy to say I'd be home late that night. "Okay, cool," he muttered over his blaring video games.

That Saturday night, my life changed forever. After the movie, Joe drove me back to my car at his place. One thing led to another, and I wound up in his bed, giving myself away to another man. My heart ached after it was over. *What just happened?* I screamed inside. *How could I have done this? I'm a youth leader, for crying out loud!*

The next morning, I went to church with Jeremy as usual. I cried through the service, tears streaming down my face as I realized what I'd done. Jeremy threw an arm around me. "You okay?" he whispered.

"Yes, sorry, I'm fine," I muttered, dying inside. Jeremy was the only man I'd ever been with when I married. I had gone from the "perfect" Christian girl to a cheating wife overnight. I'd hurt my husband, though I could not tell him what I'd done, so I kept the horrible secret tucked away and kept on singing through the worship songs.

My affair continued for more than a month. The lies began as I told Jeremy I had to work late or was going out

The Unexpected Gift

with friends; he hardly questioned me anymore. "Have fun!" he called as I slipped out of the house with a fresh coat of lipstick. My heart hurt for both of us, as I saw our relationship slowly slip away.

Joe eventually learned I was not going to leave my husband, and we broke things off. Shortly after ending things, he got fired from his job at the mall, and we didn't see each other again. Jeremy and I continued working with the youth group; I was riddled with guilt as I encouraged the kids to serve God. Meanwhile, Jeremy and I grew more and more distant. He glued himself to his video games after work, while I spent more time away from home. I was deeply saddened, wondering how we'd gotten to this place just a few months into our marriage.

Soon, a man who worked for another communications company began flirting with me. "Hey, I thought you were a goody-two-shoes girl, but I heard you changed," he drawled, sidling up to me one afternoon. "You should give me a call sometime." He winked, and I blushed. I assumed word had gotten around about Joe and me. At that moment, something inside of me gave up. Gave up on the life I'd tried so hard to live, the good-girl image I'd managed to maintain all those years, the husband who sat on the couch and hardly glanced back as I slipped out the door.

Before long, I was entangled in a second affair. Alex and I began sleeping together, and I convinced myself that I liked it, that the attention felt good, that nothing really mattered anymore. While I was giving up on the battle inside, someone was still fighting for me, though. Someone I'd given my heart to a long time ago.

One evening, I came home to find Jeremy filling a big bowl with water. "Here, sit down," he said, patting the couch. "Roll up your pant legs."

"Why?" I asked, confused.

"I want to wash your feet." He sat down and began lovingly washing my feet with warm water. I thought of the passages in the Bible where Jesus washed the disciples' dusty feet. It was an act of love, and love was what Jeremy was trying to show me now. I bit my lip, tears pricking my eyes as I wondered how loving he'd be if he knew the horrific things I'd done.

"I know things are weird right now, but our lives won't always be like this," Jeremy said softly.

A certain sadness filled my heart, and I could not find the words to reply.

One day, Jeremy left to go hang out with some friends. Relieved to have some time alone, I decided to stay home and clean. As I ran the mop over the floor, something overcame me in the quietness, and I began to sob. I put down my cleaning tools and crumbled onto the couch, bawling so hard that I could barely breathe. In that moment, God spoke to me and convicted me of my wrongdoing. He prompted me to open my Bible, and my eyes fell onto Hosea 2:7. There, I read these words: "When she runs after her lovers, she won't be able to catch them … then she will think, 'I might as well return to my husband.'" Devastated, I wept over the words until the

The Unexpected Gift

pages blurred before me as I recounted the sin I'd fallen into the last few months. I knew what I had to do next would be difficult, but it was the right thing to do.

The next day, I texted Jeremy: "I need to tell you something serious." That night when he got home, I sat him down and read him the passage from Hosea.

"Do you understand what I'm trying to tell you?" I asked with tears in my eyes.

Jeremy stared at me, his eyes wide with shock. "I …"

"I had an affair, Jeremy. Two of them, actually." I spilled everything from beginning to end, my heart aching as I forced myself to look into my husband's eyes and know the pain I was causing him. "I am so very sorry. I don't know what else to say."

"This is a lot to take in," Jeremy said quietly, looking away. "I … I just need to be left alone."

I walked away; my entire body felt like it had been crushed under a pile of bricks. I had never meant for things to come to this. All I'd ever wanted was to serve God! Inside, I felt confused, afraid and saddened by what I'd done to our marriage. I was completely broken.

Later that week, we met with our pastor, and I mustered the courage to share with him what had happened. Our pastor was devastated; we had served faithfully in the church since we had gotten married, and many of the youth looked up to us. My lies were now exposed; my actions had hurt many.

"My counsel is to separate while you try to work things out," our pastor concluded. "I'll be praying for you."

Resound

I stumbled through the next few days, going through the motions of everyday life, while my heart remained a jumbled mess. I thought of my father and the destructive path he had taken, the riptide of hurt he had caused to those closest to him because of his bad choices. For the first time in my life, I saw him with different eyes. Instead of feeling hatred toward him, I felt only compassion through my brokenness. And though a part of me had tried to blame him for my actions, God quickly humbled me, reminding me that *I* had chosen this path, not my father. Ultimately, this was between me and the Lord.

I cried out to God for forgiveness, asking him to help me reconcile my life and make things new. I sat with my father and shared that I had never forgiven him for abandoning me. He embraced me, and for the first time, he became a true father, loving and giving me direction as he should. Neither of us could take back the past, but from this moment on, we could love each other again as father and daughter. I was saddened that it had taken such devastating circumstances to get us to this place, but I was also excited for the healing journey we were about to embark on.

Things weren't so easy with Jeremy, however. Every time I saw him, he looked deflated. His eyes held no spark anymore, and his shoulders sagged. I felt helpless, half of me wanting to make things work and the rest of me wanting to call it quits. I knew Jeremy bore scars of his own from his past; his birthmother had walked out on him as a baby, and his stepmother was emotionally abusive.

The Unexpected Gift

His father was very passive and did little to defend him growing up. No wonder he had never been much of a man; no one had showed him how to be one.

One night, Alex texted again, and in a moment of weakness, I agreed to meet him. My heart screamed, "No!" but the defeated look in my husband's eyes said, "Who cares, go for it!" Before I knew it, I was sleeping with Alex again. The reignited affair led to another wave of bad choices that included partying and drinking like never before. For the first time, I truly explored the nightlife in Vegas, the City of Sin beckoning me with its tantalizing bright lights and booze.

One evening, a security guard I'd been flirting with texted me: "Do you love your husband?"

"No," I replied without thinking.

Jeremy came home and grabbed my phone. He read the text and stared at me. Neither of us knew what to say. "I'm going for a walk," he said at last.

"I'm going to take a shower," I replied, my heart racing. Something inside of me knew we were over. Any little bit of fight we both had left in us had disappeared; the scars were too deep, the disappointment too great.

When I got out of the shower, I found Jeremy on the couch, staring ahead with vacant eyes. "I called your aunt and uncle," he began. My aunt and uncle had moved back to San Diego to pastor a church. "They told me to ask you if that text was from a guy or a girl."

I took a deep breath and began to shake. "A guy," I replied slowly.

Resound

"Well, then, I have my answer." He let out a sad sigh. "They told me if it was from a guy that I should end our marriage. And so, Cathryn, I love you, but we're done."

Tears spilled down my cheeks as I saw the hurt in his eyes. "Do you want to try counseling?" I asked desperately.

He shook his head. "No."

"I am really sorry for hurting you," I said, though I knew my words could do little in that moment to ease his pain. I packed my things and left quickly, moving in with my dad until we could sort out our divorce. Less than a year after we said our vows, we dissolved them on a piece of paper and parted ways. Jeremy moved to San Diego to be with my aunt and uncle, who had become mentors to him. I could hardly blame him; a fresh start was just what he needed. But I was nearly paralyzed; suicidal thoughts briefly crossed my mind as I wondered how in the world I could ever turn my life around.

We broke our lease for our apartment, and on the last day possible, having put off the inevitable as long as I could, I went back to our place to return the key. I unlocked the apartment and took one last look around; the furniture was gone, the walls were now bare where pictures once hung. Laughter and joy had once danced in that room, a young couple's promising future displayed on the walls. But now it only held heartache, emptiness and painful memories.

I fell to the ground and wept like never before, crying out to God to redeem my life. "God, please forgive me! I'm so sorry! Please, let my life be a testimony to others someday, please use me and don't let my story go to waste," I prayed.

As I sobbed, I heard God as clearly as when I was a 12-year-old girl whisper to me in that empty room: "Daughter, everything will be okay." *Daughter!* To think that God, my heavenly father, would still use that term of endearment on a girl so broken was beautiful and humbling. I had given up on life, but he had not given up on me.

No one gets married imagining divorce. But there I was, 23, married and divorced within a year. I tried to keep my hope in God during the next few weeks, but the loneliness crept in. When Aaron, another security guard, invited me to play baseball with some friends one night, I eagerly accepted the distraction. And when he brought me back to his car after practice and made a move, I fell back into the old traps and gave myself to him.

Screw it, I thought in that moment. *I've tried to follow God my whole life, but look where I've ended up. I give up.*

My mom called not long after. "Cathryn, God spoke to me and told me we needed to get you out of Vegas. I've already bought you a plane ticket. You're coming home."

I told Aaron I was leaving town. "There's nothing more for me here," I said wearily. I hugged my father goodbye and hopped on a plane a few days later.

I returned to Oregon a broken, desperate girl. My mother took me to church one Saturday evening, where an Indian missionary who spoke stopped and prayed over my future children. I felt goose bumps prickle my spine. Deep down, I had a gut feeling I might be pregnant, but I hadn't voiced it to a soul.

My friend found me after the service. "Did you get the e-mail from my sister about the dream she had where you were pregnant?" she asked, giggling.

"That's ridiculous!" I laughed back, but inside, my stomach churned.

I stopped at Target and locked myself in a bathroom stall, where I peed on a pregnancy test and waited with shaking hands. I was only half surprised when the stick shouted back, "Yes." There I was, alone, newly divorced, starting all over in my hometown and now, carrying a child.

On instinct, I called Aaron, the only man I'd been with since my divorce.

"I'm pregnant," I sputtered.

"Cool! I'm gonna be a father!" he cried.

"Aaron, I moved back here to heal. I'm staying in Oregon," I said firmly.

"If you ain't gonna be with me, you better get an abortion!" he shouted.

I called Planned Parenthood and scheduled an abortion for the following Friday. I called several more times before my appointment, using disguised voices, trying to understand the abortion procedure.

"The doctor just goes in and vacuums out the tissue," the nurse explained flatly.

The Unexpected Gift

Tissue. Okay, so it was just tissue.

The night before my procedure, I had a vivid dream that shook me to the core. In it, I was sitting front row in an ethnically diverse crowd while a 17-year-old young man stood on a stage, preaching the gospel. "If it weren't for my mom, I wouldn't be here today," he declared. I woke up in a sweat.

"If you abort that child, you will abort future destiny," God said to me very clearly the next morning. Still shaken by the dream, I went straight to my mother and loving stepfather and confided in them.

"I already knew," she said. "God told me a while ago. Don't worry … we will never turn our backs on you."

I called my dad next; he promised to support me as well. Next, I spoke to my Uncle Ben, and he brought up adoption as a main option. "This child deserves to have a father," he said.

I sobbed every night as I lay in bed, thinking about giving up the child who already grew in my womb. Even before the ultrasound, I knew the baby was a boy. I began reading the story of Hannah and Samuel in the Bible. Hannah had given up Samuel, her only child, and trusted in the Lord for his future. Would I, too, be asked to give up my child?

My father called one day. "I really think you should name the baby Samuel," he said.

A week later, my mother echoed his thoughts. "Why do I want to keep calling the baby Sam?" she asked with a smile.

Resound

At that moment, I knew what to do. I had felt no peace about giving the baby up for adoption. I was to keep him, and I was to name him Samuel.

On May 26, 2010, a beautiful little boy named Samuel entered the world. He was the gift God had given me to help heal my heart, a reminder of his faithfulness despite my wandering ways. As I gazed into his sweet little eyes, I knew, somehow, that we were both going to be okay.

God provided for all of my needs as a single mother. I received a $3 raise at my new job and found a wonderful woman to watch Samuel for only $3 an hour while I worked. Down to the tiniest details, God proved faithful. My mother and wonderful stepfather were also a tremendous help and a huge blessing in our lives.

Having Samuel stirred up a new kind of love in my heart I didn't know was humanly possible. Despite the long nights and relentless fatigue, I was overwhelmed with peace and joy as I nursed him to sleep. Because of my broken home, I hadn't truly known what love was growing up. I had caught glimpses of it here and there, but being a mother made me realize that I had really never truly loved before. It was time to reach out to Jeremy.

I prayed and then carefully wrote Jeremy a heartfelt five-page letter expressing how sorry I was for my actions and assuring him that the demise of our marriage was not his fault. When Samuel was 3 months old, I flew to Las Vegas to visit my father, who had recently married a wonderful woman. During that visit I also flew to San Diego, contacted Jeremy and met him for coffee. There, face to face, we were able to find closure. I flew home with a peace in my heart, finally ready to move on with my life.

My Uncle Ben called me one day and told me about his friend who was starting a church in Portland. "I think you'll really like him," he encouraged me.

Pastor Luke met me for coffee on his first visit to Portland, and his friendly, sincere manner put me immediately at ease. I was the first local at Resound Church, and it was there that I found true healing and growth in my relationship with the Lord. I had never met such a grace-centered pastor before; Pastor Luke encouraged us every week to remember that it is never too late to start over with God. The kind people I met there valued me and greeted me with welcoming arms, not words of judgment. My heart softened in a way it never had before. I realized that, reeling from the pain of my past, I had become a harsh and judgmental person. But since I had been broken and now truly understood God's grace, I could extend that same grace and love to others.

I now serve at Resound Church, not with an air of pride, but with true humility. I hope to share the message of restoration in Christ with other girls who have struggled with abandonment by their fathers or perhaps shameful events that leave them believing they're not worthy of God's love.

For the first time in my life, I have a spirit of true contentment. I do not know what tomorrow holds, but I'm okay with that, for my God has taken care of me today, and that's enough for me.

Resound

Samuel is an unexpected gift; the best gift I could have received. Through him, I have learned to laugh again, to live, to love. The girl in the Target bathroom stall that day was broken, confused and afraid, but that same girl today holds her head high, knowing she is loved not only by her heavenly father, but by her earthly father as well. The cycle of hurt has been broken, and I have been made whole.

647

The Story of John
Written by Ellen R. Hale

Rap! Rap! Rap!

Someone was knocking on our front door. I scrambled from the back of the house to answer it.

Must be my roommate, Zack. He often forgets his key.

As I opened the door, three men burst into the house, two of them thrusting their guns in my face.

"Where's the weed?"

"I have no idea what you're talking about," I lied.

The two with guns threw me onto the couch and held me down, whipping their weapons across my face again and again.

"Don't play dumb — we know you got it. Where's it at?"

"You guys are wrong. There's nothing here," I insisted. "You can search the whole house."

The third man was tearing through our place. He grabbed an Xbox and $1,000 from my room. He fumbled with a laptop and left it behind.

"Where are your roommates?"

"At a friend's house a few doors down," I answered, my face stinging.

"They have anything valuable?"

"I don't know. I haven't been there much." They pushed me outside, giving me the chance to memorize the license plate number on their Chevy Caprice with glistening rims. They kept the guns pointed at me.

"You better not call the cops, or we'll kill you." They pulled away into the dark night.

I called the police right away, confident that my description of the vehicle and the robbers would lead to a quick arrest. More than an hour later, the police arrived. They collected fingerprints from inside the house and promised to investigate. They noted my bruises and black eyes. When they inquired about a motive, I told them the attack must have been random. I certainly wasn't going to tell them the truth.

The next day, I spotted the Caprice slowly driving by. I called the cops immediately, but the robbers were long gone by the time the police responded. I started to feel uneasy.

How did they know? Who told them? My roommates had been on a run back to our hometown in Oregon to pick up marijuana. They had been due back the night of the robbery, but they had been delayed. We had only told a select few about the weed. We planned to rake in $20,000 selling it to students at Arizona State.

Spooked by the robbery, my roommates decided to return to the safety we'd always known in Oregon. I tried moving in with my aunt and uncle in Phoenix and cutting ties with the friends I'd made in the two months living — and partying — there. I never discovered who ratted me out. *Would I be safe?* A month later, I headed back to Oregon, too.

647

❧❧❧

The pride of North Plains, Oregon, is the annual Elephant Garlic Festival, drawing thousands of visitors to the town of about 1,700 people. The festival features a parade, car show, craft vendors, music and lots of food, from garlic fries to garlic ice cream. The other main event in North Plains is the big garage sale on the first Saturday in May.

My family moved to North Plains in 1996, just before I turned 7 and started second grade. We lived on 3 acres surrounded by logging roads perfect for riding our family's horse. I loved riding my dirt bike so much that I built a track in one of our fields.

People from North Plains frequently identify themselves by the number "647," since those are the first three digits after the area code of every phone number in the town. I once had a baseball cap specially made with "647" on the front. Some friends sported tattoos with the numbers, while others displayed them on their dirt bikes in races. You see those numbers, you think of home.

One day, I opened the door to my father's liquor cabinet and scanned the bottles inside. The clear stuff would work best. I poured the vodka into a water bottle, then added water to the remaining vodka so that my father wouldn't notice any missing. At school, my seventh grade classmates and I sat at the lunch table in the cafeteria sipping from our water bottles and getting drunk.

My rebellious streak began at a young age. In middle

school, my friends and I sneaked out of our homes in the middle of the night searching for mischief. Drinking and smoking cigarettes followed. I discovered that the kids were willing to pay me for liquor. By ninth grade, we had moved on to smoking marijuana.

One night, I bought weed from someone I didn't know. It was laced with PCP, and my parents witnessed my bizarre behavior. The next day, I confessed what happened. They told me I shouldn't mess around with drugs again, but I didn't listen.

It's not a problem. I'll be fine.

෯෯෯

"How did you make it out here, Daniel?" One of my best friends and I had organized a party out in the country after the Friday night football game, and Daniel showed up drunk. We knew he shouldn't be driving his truck.

"Give us your keys, man."

"I'm fine!" Daniel fumed.

"You can't drive anymore. Come on."

Reluctantly, he handed the keys to Nick. I was a high school junior, and Daniel was two years older than me.

"I need the keys back," Daniel demanded later. "Just going to get the rest of the beer from my truck."

Nick eyed him suspiciously.

"I'm not going to drive," Daniel promised.

"Okay, come right back," Nick told him as he returned the keys. "You're sure you're not going to drive?"

We watched Daniel walk down the trail toward his truck. Two other people appeared to be waiting inside the truck for him.

Sure enough, we heard the engine starting. They took off down the road.

"Great." Nick sighed. "He better come back. Maybe he's screwing with us."

Half an hour later, Daniel had not returned. We walked down the road until we reached a point where we had cell phone service. Daniel didn't answer his phone. We continued walking and reached a bend in the road where we could see a mile away down in the valley. Ambulance lights flashed and a helicopter approached for landing. We recognized Daniel's truck.

The party broke up, and I fell asleep uneasily at Nick's house. The next morning, his phone rang. Daniel was dead.

My stomach sank. *No! This has to be a dream. How could this happen to someone we know?* I had driven drunk myself many times.

We found out that Daniel was driving 90 miles per hour when he collided with an oncoming vehicle. He died instantly, and his two passengers were on life support in the ICU.

Everyone blamed Nick and me. They thought Daniel would be alive if not for us. Our friends wouldn't even look at us, and we struggled with guilt. *What if we had kept the keys? What if we had walked with him to the truck instead of believing him?*

Resound

My parents supported me, insisting that Daniel alone bore responsibility.

"It's not your fault," they assured me. "Even the guys in the truck let him drive. You can't blame yourself anymore."

≈≈≈≈

An advertisement caught my eye on campus at Portland Community College, where I took some classes during high school. A company sought people to train and hire as disc jockeys. I responded to the ad and started spinning tunes at school dances, weddings and other special events.

My friends and I now used cocaine as our drug of choice. I thrived on the energy boost from the high, which made life seem fun and exciting.

Once I found a reliable dealer, I began using daily. Although I needed a fix before school just to function, I never considered that I had a problem.

Since I earned good money from my DJ job, I bought larger amounts of cocaine and sold it. Tons of kids from high school wanted the drug. Word spread quickly to call me.

From there, I began dealing ecstasy. The money came so easily, I felt like I supported my addiction for free. The cash kept coming, so I never had to take a break from using or resort to stealing. I indulged in new clothing and expensive stereos for my car.

Standing at the sink in the bathroom during a rock concert, I reached into my pocket for the drugs I'd brought to sell. Just then, a security guard walked in.

"What is that?" he barked.

"I don't know what you're talking about." I feigned innocence.

The guard searched me, discovered the bags, handcuffed me and led me outside past my friends, who quickly dispersed. A fight broke out nearby, demanding the guard's attention. He unlocked the cuffs and shoved me out the door, warning me not to come back.

After that, I added a level of security in such situations by enlisting go-betweens. I paid them $100 to help sell the drugs. I collected a few thousand dollars in one night, making their fee plenty worthwhile.

જ્જ્જ્

Techno music blared and laser lights flashed as I waded into the crowd at another rave. Girls dressed in neon colors and fishnet stockings bumped against me as they danced. Security guards looked the other way as people slapped $10 bills in my hand in return for a pill of ecstasy. The party swirled until sunrise.

I had graduated from high school and returned to Hillsboro after my brief stint living in Phoenix. Nothing else had changed. I remained John the drug dealer.

At home, my phone vibrated. I glanced at the text message.

Resound

"You got any blue dolphins?" I knew this guy, so I texted back.

"How many do you want?"

Soon, he came to my apartment to pick them up. I retreated inside to wait for the next message to arrive.

෧෧෧

"John, do you believe in God?" Lauren asked.

Lauren and I had been dating for a month when the subject of our conversation turned to religion. I hesitated. *What would she think of my answer?*

"I've always considered myself an atheist," I explained. "I don't believe in God."

"Oh, I do. I don't necessarily think people need to go to church, but I believe in God. Someone had to create this world. It didn't just show up on its own."

I had only attended church a few times growing up. My father had been raised Catholic and never practiced as an adult. Our family never discussed religion. When I attended church with a friend, I didn't understand anything. The topic didn't come up often among my circle of friends through the years, but if it did, I told others I was an atheist.

I met Lauren through her sister, a co-worker of mine at 24-Hour Fitness. Lauren was everything I wanted — beautiful, smart and fun. She had participated in national debate competitions; she had been elected homecoming queen.

When she left to go to college 14 hours away in Montana on a full scholarship, we vowed to stay together. I couldn't imagine my life without her. Still, a lack of trust soon surfaced.

I knew Lauren was attending a concert with friends and wouldn't answer my texts. But when I saw photos of her with guys on Facebook, I started asking questions. She began questioning me when I hung out with my friends. We realized that our feelings hadn't changed, but we couldn't continue our relationship because of the distance.

My roommate, Ryan, noticed how bummed I felt over our breakup. I appreciated living with Ryan, who didn't do drugs and rarely drank, after my previous roommate was arrested and I kicked him out. I didn't need the police snooping around where I lived.

"Look, John, I know you're going through a lot of stuff with drugs and alcohol and Lauren," Ryan said. "I think you should come to church with me."

"I'm not sure," I replied.

I didn't know much about Christianity, but I thought Christians were boring and stuck up. *How can they have any fun with all those rules? Who would want that kind of lifestyle?*

Still, something stirred inside me at Ryan's invitation. On Sunday, August 29, 2010, we walked into Solid Rock Church together. Unsure of what to expect, I found a seat. I overheard a woman sitting nearby talking about her concern for her daughter's direction in life and how she'd been praying for God to show her daughter what path to follow. God certainly seemed real to her. She didn't sound like she thought she was perfect. She sounded like she believed God would take care of her problems.

The guest speaker that morning was a man named Andrew Palau. During his sermon, I learned that his father was a famous pastor and author, Luis Palau, who traveled the world speaking about salvation through faith in Jesus. Yet Andrew Palau didn't believe the message his father preached. He attended the University of Oregon and partied hard.

He sounded a lot like me.

But Andrew Palau eventually left his old ways behind at age 27, became a Christian and started serving God. Now, he preaches at churches like Solid Rock and festivals all around the United States and other countries, too.

Back at home after the service, I sat in front of my laptop and cried. *I'm not going anywhere in life. I can't keep selling drugs forever — I'll end up dead or in jail. It's a miracle I've never been arrested. It's not right how I've been living.*

I contemplated praying, but I didn't know what to say. I didn't know if God was really there with me in the room and would listen or if he was far away and wouldn't care. I logged in to Facebook and scanned my friends' recent posts.

A Bible verse caught my eye. A few minutes later, another friend posted a single word: "God."

This is strange. My friends never talk about God. All they care about is having fun.

Another post popped up on the screen. "God! God! God!"

I stumbled to my bed and dropped to my knees. *God, I believe you're real. But I'm confused. I don't know what to do or where to go from here. Please give me direction.*

Wiping tears from my eyes, I looked at the clock on my nightstand. It read 6:47, immediately reminding me of home and a time before I was hooked on drugs and hooked on making money, a time before the only calls I received came from people wanting their next fix.

Just then, my cell phone buzzed. This text message said "I love you." My dad sent it.

I needed to go to North Plains right away. I had been so rebellious, and yet here was my dad telling me he loved me!

After a half-hour drive, I stepped into my parents' home. Seated at the table, my dad began crying when he saw me.

"You know, John, I had a girlfriend in high school who I thought was perfect. I just knew she was the one. But it didn't work out," Dad said. "And you know what? I'm grateful every day that we didn't stay together because I met your mom, and we had two of the best kids anyone could ever have." His eyes teared up.

"Lauren and I broke up," I admitted. "I've been taking it really hard. Like you just said, I thought she was the one. But you know what, Dad? I attended church today, and I was praying when you sent your text message. And I'm wondering — why did you text 'I love you'?"

Resound

"I don't know." He shrugged. "I just felt like I needed to let you know."

So no explanation existed, except for God. *Could it be that he loves me even more than my dad does?*

At 5 a.m. on Sunday morning, I pulled myself out of bed. It's time to help Resound Church get ready for its two worship services, held in a movie theater. Shortly after the night I prayed for the first time, I was introduced to Resound Church and found a new life. I haven't used drugs since the night I prayed for the first time. It hasn't been easy, but I found Bible verses such as these to see me through times of temptation:

> For I have the desire to do what is good, but I cannot carry it out. For I do not do the good I want to do, but the evil I do not want to do — this I keep on doing. Now if I do what I do not want to do, it is no longer I who do it, but it is sin living in me that does it … What a wretched man I am! Who will rescue me from this body that is subject to death? Thanks be to God, who delivers me through Jesus Christ our Lord" (Romans 7:18-20, 24-25).

When a friend asked me to celebrate his 21st birthday with him, I thought having a beer with him at a bar would be harmless. But afterward, we headed back to his place, and I walked into a far too familiar scene. The guys offered me cocaine. Even a year earlier, I wouldn't have hesitated to join in. But now, I bolted for the door and left. I couldn't linger a moment while people used drugs. God would have given me the strength to withstand the temptation, but I didn't want to risk displeasing him in any way. That night, I realized I needed to make a complete break with my past.

God has provided forgiveness for my sins, instead of the punishment I deserve, through the death and resurrection of Jesus. I feel a happiness I didn't know existed that pales in comparison to the fleeting high of drugs and alcohol. I realize my "friends" didn't really value me, they valued what I had. At church, I've made genuine friends who want nothing from me at all.

After 20 years of not believing in God, I harbor no doubts that he saved me, that Jesus is alive and that I am loved beyond my comprehension. Deep down, I always knew a void existed in my heart. The truth is, God was missing all along.

I love Resound Church and the opportunities I have to serve the Lord. There is no place I'd rather be. I spent so many years leading people on a path toward addiction and destruction, and now I have the opportunity to guide them toward a life of freedom and abundance. My life no longer revolves around money. God has totally changed my heart.

I pray for God to use me in the future, as I sense him calling me to minister to young adults. So many young people are lost, as I was, and desperately need the forgiveness God offers to all. I have the chance to use my experience to reach out to others. No one, no matter how far from God he is or how low he feels, is beyond rescue. There is always light at the end of the tunnel.

༉ ༉ ༉

It was Sunday. A normally outgoing woman walked into Resound Church. I recognized immediately that she was high on meth. Not many people would notice the signs, but I am well-acquainted with them. She didn't talk to anyone. I had heard she had unfortunately started hanging around the wrong friends who were addicted to meth and heroin. When I greeted her, she refused to look me in the eyes. She appeared lifeless.

Later that day, I gave her a call.

"Listen, I know you weren't sober at church today," I said.

"Yeah, I wasn't," she admitted. Then she shared her struggles with me. We talked for several hours, as I told her my story and the Bible verses that have helped me stay clean. "The path you're on doesn't lead to anything good, trust me," I said.

After multiple conversations over a few months, she stopped using and turned away from that crowd.

I know many more like her are waiting for their moment of salvation. Mine happened at 6:47 on a Sunday night, and I haven't been the same since.

Awakening
The Story of Rita Vater
Written by Marty Minchin

My long burgundy dress swished around my legs as I took my place on the risers with my church's youth choir. Jack had made me paint the entire exterior of our four-bedroom house in the blazing Arizona heat to earn the money to buy that dress, which I had worn for summer choir tour performances in California.

Today wasn't a typical choir performance. We were singing to honor the memory of Jack, my controlling, mean stepfather, who had died earlier that week of a heart attack. Someone at the church thought it would be a good idea for the youth choir to sing at his memorial service, so here I was.

The congregation was small; my family changed churches every few years, and we hadn't been at this one very long. My mother — who was 32 years old and eight months pregnant — my three younger sisters and my 2-year-old half brother sat stoically on a pew.

A microphone loomed in front of me. Moments earlier, a few people had spoken into it about how good a man Jack was. Those people didn't know that what they said wasn't true.

I couldn't take my eyes off that microphone. Everything in me wanted to break rank with the choir and step up to the device that would magnify my voice many times over. My words would carry to the farthest corners of that sanctuary, announcing to these deceived people who Jack really was. A child molester. A cruel and angry parent. A man who had turned my fun-loving mother into an emotionless robot. A stepfather who had visited my bedroom many nights …

Oh, if I only had the guts.

But I was 15 years old and a quiet girl, and I stayed quiet that day. I sang the song with the choir and sat down.

❧❧❧

My real father was a military man, an E-6 in the U.S. Army. He and my mom married young, had four daughters and moved every two years. I made friends easily, but I quickly learned to keep my distance because they would only be my friends until we moved to our next location.

Dad was gruff and harsh. He wasn't a lot of fun. When I was young, he treated me like a boy. I have many pictures of myself as a baby wearing t-shirts and jeans. He never made me feel like I was a disappointment to him, though. In fact, I believed I was his favorite.

Because I was the oldest, by the time I was 9 years old, I was the only one of my sisters who could come home from school by myself. Many times, Dad would be home in the afternoons because he worked odd shifts, and we would be alone.

Awakening

Our house was strewn with *Playboy* magazines. My dad was always reading them, which I thought was normal.

"Come here, Rita," he said to me one day, a *Playboy* rolled up in one hand. "You want to take a nap?"

Of course I did. I savored the secret feeling that my dad loved me best. "Crawl up," he said, lying down on the couch and motioning to his upper body. I settled down on his broad chest, and I could hear his heart beating and his lungs filling with air as he breathed. As I dozed off, he lifted the *Playboy* magazine over my head and began to read.

కింకింకి

Mom and Dad divorced when I was 11 years old and we were living in Germany. Dad had an affair with my mother's best friend, a woman I used to babysit for. He eventually married her. Mom, my sisters and I moved to Phoenix and in with my grandparents in their two-bedroom house. My mom took a job as a secretary, and not long after, she married her boss, Jack.

Jack was the first Christian I had ever met. He was 57, older than my grandparents, and he sold houses. Mom and Jack bought a brand-new house in suburban Phoenix furnished with model-home furniture. Jack carried a Bible around and made us pray at mealtimes. He also made us go to church.

At home, Jack was controlling. He would force us to

eat food at the table. If we needed money or wanted to go somewhere, we were required to ask Jack. When my parents were married, I talked to my mom if I needed anything. Now Jack was the doorkeeper, both literally and figuratively.

Jack and my mom spent most nights in their room with the door shut, watching TV. The night I started my period for the first time, I was desperate to talk to my mom, so I stood outside their room and gently knocked.

The door cracked open, and Jack peered out, his spindly arms and legs framing his potbellied torso. He was the last person I wanted to talk to about such a personal matter.

"I need to talk to my mom," I said as calmly as I could. I could see my mom lying on the bed behind him, and I was sure she could hear me.

"What do you need to talk to her about?"

"I just need to talk to her, okay?" I glared at him, willing my mom to get up and override this ridiculous conversation.

Jack paused, savoring his position of power. "Oh, did you start your period?"

How did he know? My eyes teared up, and I looked down. "Yes," I replied. "I really need to talk to my mom."

Life felt out of control. I couldn't even have a conversation with my mom without getting this awful man's approval first. I hated him.

ॐॐॐ

Awakening

It wasn't long before Mom was pregnant with her fifth child, and she wasn't even 30 years old. The night that Mom was laboring in the hospital, Jack, who had stayed home for some reason, knocked on my bedroom door.

Our white carpet had been dyed brown that day, and I woke up to the sound of Jack creeping into my room and a heavy wet carpet smell filling my nostrils. I opened my eyes, groggy from waking from a deep sleep.

"Jack?" I whispered. "What are you doing in here?" Fear coursed through me.

This was the late 1970s, an age before cable television and MTV. I didn't know about sex and what led up to it. All I knew was that my mom's husband was in my room in the middle of the night, and I wasn't sure what he wanted.

"I love you, Rita," he cajoled. I could smell his putrid breath, the result of a medical condition. "Come on, Rita. I don't want to have sex with you because you'd get pregnant. Just let me get in your bed."

His hands groped under my sheets and blanket, and I pushed and shoved his octopus arms away, hissing at him to get out of my room. I kept my voice low so my sisters wouldn't hear. He tried to kiss me all over as I squirmed into a ball.

Finally, my efforts paid off, and Jack slunk out of the room.

Should I tell? A million thoughts raced through my mind as I pulled the covers tightly up to my neck. The image that won out was that of my mom in the hospital with her new baby boy, soon to come home to four daughters and Jack. I knew that if Jack left, she couldn't take care of all five of us by herself.

I can't tell her. She just had a baby. If I tell her, she'll have to leave him, and how is she going to do that?

I kept quiet.

~ ~ ~

After Mom brought baby Arthur home, Jack still snuck into my room about once a week, and I would push him away until he left. I finally asked my sister Raunda to sleep in my room, and Jack stayed away as long as she was there.

When Raunda got tired of sleeping on my floor and announced she was moving back into her room, I broke down and spilled my secret about Jack. I begged her not to tell our mom, and she agreed to stay in my room and keep the information to herself.

Those nights in my room, Jack had pleaded with me to let him touch me, sometimes offering me money to do things to him. He would insist that he loved me. During the day, he was awful and mean, often making veiled sexual comments. He would say things like, "You have a lot of pimples, no one is ever going to love you." He would tell me that my shorts were too tight, and he could see everything. If I were in the hallway and not walking fast enough, he would shove me out of the way.

One day Jack and Raunda got in a fight, and she told our mom about Jack's nighttime visits. Jack said that

Awakening

wasn't a very nice thing to lie to my mother about, and I moved in with a family from our home church for my sophomore year in high school.

I lived across town and saw my family on the weekend, usually at church. When I returned home for my junior year, one of Jack's daughters had moved in, figured out he was molesting my kindergarten-aged sister Roxie and called Child Protective Services.

Jack never was removed from our house. Instead, we all went to therapy together.

I sat in the corner of the room in a chair as the therapist talked to Mom and Jack. I never talked, and I was never talked to.

That was family counseling.

❧❧❧

Less than two years after Arthur was born, my mom was pregnant again.

"You have to forgive me," Jack said one evening when we were alone. "The Bible says so."

I looked at him, incredulous. This hypocritical man who had never once apologized for anything he had done to me and my sister, who treated us like he was our slave master, wanted me to forgive him? What a joke.

Jack leaned back in his chair and crossed his arms over his chest, waiting for me to agree with his proclamation. He looked so old with his rickety body and nearly bald head.

Resound

A feeling of control swept through me as I realized I could say no. I *wanted* to say no.

"I can't do it," I told him, looking him right in the eyes. "You can't make me forgive you."

And I meant it.

అహ్ అహ్ అహ్

Finally, my mom was taking me to get my learner's permit. A license would grant me some freedom, the ability to get out of the stifling environment of home — even for a little while — where Jack wouldn't even let us out of the front yard to hang out with our neighborhood friends.

Mom and I climbed into our blue two-door Honda Civic on a hot Phoenix afternoon and stopped to pick up something at her office before heading to the DMV.

With four siblings, it was hard to get time alone with my mom, and today I had her all to myself for this important event.

The phone rang as soon as we walked into her building.

"You need to come home," the voice told her. "Something has happened to someone at your house, and you need to come home right now."

I sighed. *Are you kidding me?* It was always something. I was never going to get my permit.

As we pulled up in front of the house, we were greeted by a lone police officer standing in our yard. The officer

Awakening

ushered my mom inside out of the 120-degree heat to break the news.

Jack was very involved in church activities, and that afternoon while driving to a church function, he had a massive heart attack. He hit another car, which happened to be driven by a physician. The doctor performed CPR on the spot, but Jack didn't make it.

My mom emerged from the house, hot and wilted and swollen with her eight-months-pregnant belly. She was so plain standing there, no makeup and a light-brown permed Afro. This woman was a far cry from the woman who had worn go-go boots and miniskirts not too many years before.

Mom didn't cry.

I didn't, either. Instead, happiness overwhelmed me.

Jack may have stopped coming into my bedroom, but he hadn't stopped being mean, even after he got caught. He never stopped controlling my mom, telling her when she could wear makeup, ordering her not to shave her armpits or telling her how to fix her hair. Mom used to be fun and full of life, full of dreams for her career. That day, she was too numb inside to squeeze out a tear. She was 32 years old, a widow and about to have her sixth child.

How much can one person take? I thought.

My mind turned to God. I finally had something to thank him for. *If there really is a God, Jack's death is all the proof I need.*

After Jack's memorial service, we had no more need for church. Except for my sister Rosie, who loved church and had a sincere commitment to God, we all stopped going.

৵৵৵৵

Jack had kept a tight rein on us. When he was home, he rarely let us out of the house, and we had to ask him for everything. My freshman year in high school, I chose to fail a home economics project rather than ask Jack for the money to buy supplies for it. Normally, I was a straight-A student.

I came up with all sorts of devious ways to get around Jack's iron fist. He sold cookware for a while and would be gone at night at dinner parties, and I would sneak out and run wild, partying, smoking pot and drinking. I didn't really have friends because of my confinement, but I had plenty of hookups. I met boys in the neighborhood and at school. They would come to my room when my parents were out, we'd have sex and they'd leave. I had no emotion about it.

One day soon after Jack's death, our next-door neighbor's grandson came to visit from California. His reputation preceded him. Jimmy and his band had been on *The Gong Show* and won, and his family frequently bragged about Jimmy and his manager and his band's recording contract.

I was intrigued by this long-haired rocker who was eight years older than me and was the talk of the neighborhood girls. When he showed up in my front yard

Awakening

and asked if he could play our grand piano, I welcomed him into the living room and listened as he reeled off song after song. I pushed my blond Farah Fawcett hair away from my face and leaned into the music.

He was 22 years old. I was barely 15.

All I knew of boys was one-night stands, and Jimmy was different. He was a man, and he sensed that I was unhappy. He was interested, and he wanted to rescue me.

We beat a trail between our houses, getting together for sex and to smoke pot. He had a car and a job, and he bought me stuff. We dreamed of moving to California, away from all of my family complexities in Phoenix.

Soon I started to feel sick so often that my mom took me to our pediatrician. Without telling my mom, the nurse ran a pregnancy test and called me with the positive results.

"You need to tell your mom," the nurse told me. But I couldn't tell her. Jimmy could go to jail for having sex with a 15 year old. I felt scared and stuck. I decided to protect Jimmy and have an abortion, so he drove me to a Planned Parenthood clinic.

The abortion would cost $110, an enormous sum for an unemployed high school student. Planned Parenthood, however, arranged a loan for me. Meanwhile, the nurse from the pediatrician's office kept calling.

The night before my abortion appointment, the phone rang. It was the nurse, again.

"I can't put my mom through one more thing," I told

her. "I can just take care of this, and she won't even have to know about it."

I hung up and sat on my bed and stared at the wall for a while. The gravity of my situation weighed heavily.

I don't think I can do this. If Jimmy has to go to jail, he has to go to jail. My pregnancy suddenly felt romantic. *We produced this life. How can I do this to a product of our love?*

෨෨෨

During my junior year of high school, I was the only pregnant girl in my school. I felt bad for my mom, who now had a pregnant teenage daughter on top of her own infant and children.

I graduated with my high school senior class, and Jimmy and I got an apartment. He worked at a car wash, and I took care of Ryan, who has retinitis pigmentosa, a genetic eye disease that leads to incurable blindness. It was all very exciting, like playing house. My domestic fantasy lasted about a month.

We quickly ran out of money. Jimmy was gone all the time playing bass guitar at bars where I was too young to get in the door. He became super protective of me, threatened by anything that might take my attention — including Ryan. He didn't even like me to read books to our son. Jimmy was mean to Ryan, too. "Get out of my way, you little ba*****," he'd say if Ryan blocked his path.

My relationship and my son forced me to put aside my

Awakening

dreams of college and becoming a nurse. But I needed a job, so I got a certification as a medical assistant and went to work for a Planned Parenthood birth control center.

When Ryan was 5, I walked down the aisle and married Jimmy at the church by my mom's house.

Do you really think being married is going to change anything? I asked myself as I looked at Jimmy waiting at the altar. But I wasn't going to move back in with my mom; she had remarried, and I refused to live with another stepfather.

One night, when Jimmy was out, I sat in our living room in our seedy little rental house. It was filled with roaches and grime, and the mottled shag carpets were stained a hundred shades of brown. Ryan, so cute with his Coke-bottle-bottom glasses and brown hair, sat cross-legged on that disgusting carpet, inches from the TV console.

I fought the urge to pick him up and run.

How could you let your baby sit on that floor?

It hit me then that even adults don't have control over their lives. I had nowhere to go. I was estranged from my family, and I had no friends. Adults, I realized, don't always get to live the life they want.

For me, that meant there was nothing I could do but try to survive the choices I had made and do the best I could with my son.

And that's what I did.

❧❧❧

Resound

In 1988, Jimmy and I moved to Montana, where his parents had relocated to open a restaurant. We would help them out, and I was overjoyed at the opportunity for a fresh start in such a beautiful place. Finally, we could end the cycle of moving constantly to get away from bill collectors, of Jimmy struggling to keep a job.

I loved Montana. There, I decided we should have another baby, this time one who was planned from the beginning.

Rheanna was born in 1990 when Ryan was in first grade. I cried every day of my pregnancy with Ryan; with Rheanna, I was determined her birth would be a joyous event.

But soon the same old routines took over. I got a job and kept it, while Jimmy switched jobs and we moved between rental houses and apartments. We made it five years before Jimmy couldn't get a job in that small Montana town, and we moved back to Phoenix.

Once there, life began to look up again.

Jimmy's uncle had let us take over the payments on his beautiful suburban house. It had four bedrooms, carpeted floors and a big backyard.

Finally, we would live in a house, *our house.* We would stay here and grow roots — as long as Jimmy could keep a job and we could keep up with the mortgage payments. Money was always tight with us.

∾∾∾

Awakening

The phone rang one Saturday morning before we were even dressed. It was the police, who were at my mother's house.

"You need to find your parents," the officer insisted. "Your little brothers are here, but we can't find them. Your sister Roxie has been in an accident."

Jimmy found Mom and Dad, who had strangely reconciled after years of divorce, at the grocery store. They drove home, tossed the grocery bags in the front yard and sped to the hospital.

A police officer met us there and told us Roxie's boyfriend was being questioned at the station, but it didn't look like he was involved.

My mind spun. "What are you talking about?" I asked. "Roxie was in a car accident."

"Didn't you know?" The cop looked at me quizzically. "It was a shooting accident."

Roxie endured a difficult childhood. She was pregnant at ages 12 and 14, and although it was never spoken, we all knew the father was my uncle. She gave the children up for adoption, got her GED and became a medical assistant. She was planning to marry one of her instructors.

Recently, Roxie had received a letter from the State of Arizona stating that her son, who she assumed had been adopted, had bounced between foster homes for 10 years. He had learning disabilities and was blind in one eye, and finally, a family wanted to adopt him. Roxie had kept her children a secret, and now she was face to face with her past.

Resound

That Saturday morning, Roxie sat alone in her house, picked up a gun and shot herself in the eye. She didn't leave a note, and we never saw her alive again.

Driving to her funeral the Friday after Thanksgiving, we passed the mall on the way to the cemetery. The parking lot was packed with cars, people shopping on the busiest shopping day of the year.

Life is going on, and we're dying here, I thought as I stared blankly out the window. *This is the worst day of our lives, and people don't even know. Really, our lives are nothing in the great scheme of the world.*

❧❧❧

Not surprisingly, our newfound home stability didn't last long. Jimmy played baseball, and one night he broke his leg badly during a game and had to have surgery. He was out of work for a long time, and we lost the house and had to move in with my parents in Phoenix.

The *Playboy* magazines were back, and my dad was up to his old tricks. I could hear him padding around late at night, then the familiar tones of the computer modem making a connection to the Internet. I felt sad for him because I knew what he was up to.

Every year, my sister Rosie, who had never stopped going to church, guilted me into attending a mother-daughter banquet at her church. By this time, I had become a clone of my mom. I was functional, but I was numb inside, void of emotion. When my kids would play or do something cute, I felt nothing. *That's not normal,* I would tell myself. *Mothers are supposed to have feelings about their kids, and I don't have any.*

When Rosie and I walked into the banquet, my third in a row, people remembered me and talked to me. They were friendly and kind, and I saw something in them that I wanted my kids to have.

But my life was a far cry from theirs. The day in and day out of dealing with Jimmy's anger, unemployment and constant lying was taking a toll. Every weekend, I drank the days away because we had nothing else to do. I had no hobbies, friends or money.

Maybe it was time we started going to church.

࿇࿇࿇

My kids hated church that first Sunday. Ryan was a sophomore in high school, and Rheanna was 7, and I made them go to youth group and children's activities.

But they were soon drawn into the church's community, and the more they loved it, the more I hated it. I started looking at the people in church and thinking, *This has got to be fake. Nobody can be this happy and joyful.*

Their house would burn down, and they'd praise the Lord. I could never be like that.

One Sunday, a lady convinced me to step forward to the altar when the pastor asked if anyone would like to pray to become a Christian. I had warmed up to the people in church, so I inched out of my pew. *I've tried everything else, and if this isn't real, then nothing's real,* I told myself as I walked to the front of the church. *I'll give it a shot.*

I prayed the words of the sinner's prayer, acknowledging that I needed Jesus to forgive me of my sins and live in my heart. But I felt nothing.

Some people have dramatic conversions when they become Christians, but mine was a long and steady journey. I would meet people, long for the joy that Christ had brought to their lives and become their shadow. If they went to a class, I went to the class. I wanted what they had.

But sometimes I felt like I had to get saved every week. *Please God,* I would beg. *Make it real this time. I really want it. I want to be a new creation, but every week when I go home, nothing changes.*

Finally, a lady at church sat me down and said something that made sense.

"Rita, your spirit is new, but your soul has to be restored," she told me. "It's a process."

Why didn't someone tell me this to start with?

ಹಿಂಡಿ

Jimmy felt threatened by church at first, but after a while, he began attending and became a Christian. Finally! I truly hoped that God would restore my marriage and life would be good.

Awakening

My faith was growing as I prayed, read the Bible and attended church. In Sunday school, I was the one who raised my hand with questions. I *needed* this to be real, and it was. God was meeting me there.

As usual, though, nothing changed at home, and this time it got worse.

In 2003, we hosted people from church for Thanksgiving lunch. Jimmy and I got into an argument that morning, and he took off for six hours. We ate without him, and he was fuming that we hadn't waited for him. He pouted in the bedroom while I washed the dishes, then I grabbed my keys to run to the store.

Jimmy flew out of the apartment building after me, wildly motioning for me to roll down the car window. I did, and then I reeled back as his hand shot in and slapped me.

"Where do you think you're going, you b****?" he screamed, inches from the car. "Get out of that car and back in the house now!"

"Jimmy, I have to get something at the store." My voice was unnaturally calm. "I'll be back in 10 minutes."

That was not what he wanted to hear. Once again his face loomed in the open window, and I snapped my head back in shock as he spit on me. I pressed the button to raise the window and peeled out of the parking lot. At the store, tears dropped off my cheeks as I walked up and down the aisles.

That night, I decided that I was done with Jimmy, but worse things would happen before I told him to leave.

Resound

Jimmy was addicted to painkillers, and he had long been stealing and lying to pay for his habit. I found pawnshop receipts in our house, and he would tell me he had sold items he'd picked up at yard sales. When my dad couldn't find his power saw and the sound equipment went missing from our church, I put two and two together.

The last straw was when Ryan came home from a summer internship and couldn't find his drum set, which we'd been storing for him. I knew immediately what had happened.

After 23 years with Jimmy, I made him leave. He didn't argue. He didn't even look me in the eye as he packed his things.

Our divorce was final in December, and I vowed to never marry again.

Jimmy was soon convicted of credit card and identity theft and went to jail. He's been incarcerated on and off since.

かかか

"John and Paul can't join my small group," I insisted to a church leader. "This is not a good idea. I'm a single woman, and I don't want single guys in our group. I don't like it."

I had become a small group leader in my church, and I was one seminar away from being credentialed as an Assemblies of God minister — a position not open to remarried people. In our church, people were assigned to small groups, and I was determined that John and Paul should go elsewhere.

As life would have it, though, the two men joined my group. I asked other church leaders to make sure I was never left alone with them, but as our group spent more time together, I couldn't help becoming close friends with both of them. We felt like a little family.

John became an especially good friend. In group meetings, we seemed to have our own conversations. Since he was dating someone else and I was never going to get married, though, our friendship was safe.

❧❧❧

In 2006, my tough biker dad was diagnosed with cancer, and he got very sick very fast.

Dad wasn't into God. He would get argumentative whenever we brought him up, but as he lay on his hospital bed recovering from brain surgery, I felt like my pastor should come see him.

I listened in amazement as my dad told the pastor that when he was in high school, he wanted to be a minister. But for some reason his church's leadership told him he couldn't, and Dad never went back to church.

"Do you know where you are going to be in eternity?" the pastor asked gently. "Do you want to ask Jesus into your heart?"

"Yes!" my dad replied in his strained voice.

Resound

Holy cow.

The pastor put his hand on my dad's bony shoulder, and they prayed. Dad began shaking and sobbing, and even though he was hooked up to wires and tubes, he slid out of bed and onto his knees. He clutched the pastor's Bible to his chest, buried his bearded face in the side of the bed and shook and cried for 15 minutes.

"I'm sorry, I'm sorry," he wept over and over.

It was the most amazing transformation I've ever seen. God's presence filled that room and changed everything. My cheeks were wet with tears, and I wished that Rosie, my faithful sister, could have been there.

A plan formed in my mind. What a testimony this would be! Dad would come home, get better and come to church with us. The next day, I bought him a Bible with his name engraved on the cover. Rosie bought him a big necklace with a cross that would fit his biker style. But Dad never wore that necklace, and he never opened the Bible. He was barely conscious again.

A month later, with worship music playing softly in the background in his bedroom at home, my dad went to be with God. It was February 10th, my daughter's birthday.

We held a little party for her at my parents' house, ate birthday cake and visited with Dad, who was there under Hospice care. He had opened his eyes that morning and told my mom that he loved her; he had been unresponsive since.

His breaths came farther and farther apart.

"It's okay, Dad," I whispered to him, holding his hand.

Awakening

"We'll take care of Mom. You can see Jesus. Just walk away with him. Go be with Jesus."

For a long time, he didn't take another breath. Then he was with God.

My siblings who weren't Christians cried and carried on, but I felt an overwhelming peace. I had the privilege of watching my dad walk into eternity, saved at the last hour by God's grace and mercy, and it was beautiful.

 જે જે જે

When my dad died, I felt no unforgiveness toward him despite the inappropriate things he had done to me as a child. Next to Jack, my dad looked like a saint.

Jack was a different story. Long after he died, the mention of his name caused a well of hatred to swell up inside of me, almost choking me with its power. If Jack was in heaven, even after I became a Christian, I wasn't sure I wanted to go there with him. I could feel the weight of my unforgiveness toward Jack dragging on me and keeping me from truly becoming a new and free person. If I forgave Jack, however, I felt like it would minimize what he had done to my family and me.

Jack wasn't the only problem. There was the kind elderly doctor I worked for who tried to assault me in the empty office. There was Jimmy, who had emotionally abused me for decades.

"Jack might be in heaven," my pastor told me when I met with him to talk about my lingering unforgiveness.

Resound

"That's God's grace. But you, Rita, are a daughter of God."

As my pastor looked up, I saw tears on his face.

"On behalf of all men, I ask you to forgive us," he said.

I didn't forgive Jack that day, but for the first time I *wanted* to forgive him. Every day after, I reminded myself that God was the judge and that I had forgiven these men. Like the restoration of my soul, forgiveness was a process.

I learned that forgiveness was all about my own heart — it had nothing to do with the other person. We can't afford to not forgive people, because it taints your life and fills you with anger and bitterness.

ॐॐॐ

I gained a lot of weight during my divorce, expanding to 215 pounds and a size 16. One day, John and I got into a conversation about fitness and exercise. "I've put on weight to keep men away from me," I blurted out, surprising myself with my words. That was partially true. I also could go out with friends for the first time in my life, and all of that eating at restaurants was showing.

God, I prayed. *What's going on? I don't want to be unhealthy and hide behind something.*

God began working on my heart, which until that day had been happy to be single while all of my single girlfriends longed to be married.

It's okay to want to be married, God spoke to me. *I put desires in the hearts of women to be married and taken care of.*

Awakening

Our small group decided that we would get healthy together, and we outlined a 12-week exercise regime and diet plan that we would hold each other accountable to. I planned to win.

John was already in great shape, but he wanted to help us. We'd meet at the high school and run up the bleachers and do other exercises. Our small group members, however, dropped out one by one until it was just John and me. We'd work out at his gym or sit by his pool and talk.

I eventually lost 80 pounds — and gained a husband.

ふふふ

John and I married in 2008. Having a godly husband is better than I ever imagined. Before I loved John, most importantly, I *liked* him.

We moved to Portland in 2010 for John's job, leaving our grown children and a job I'd held for 17 years. While looking for a church, we found information about Resound Church online.

Here was a church starting up, and I had always been envious of people who had been part of a church since it began in their pastor's living room. I thought it was the coolest thing, and here was my chance to get on board with a new church.

"We're not making any commitments today," John told me as we walked into a coffee shop to meet with Luke Reid, pastor of Resound Church.

Resound

As we sat around that little table in the corner of the coffee shop, we listened to Luke speak our language about church. John and I knew this church was right before we'd even spoken a word between us.

"We're in," John told Luke as we wrapped up our conversation. A huge smile spread across my face. So much for not making any decisions today.

ॐ ॐ ॐ

On a recent Sunday, our Resound congregation lined up around an indoor pool at a hotel. Pastor Luke, wearing a black t-shirt, climbed into the water and baptized three people, including two from our small group.

A worship team member brought a guitar, and we sang and prayed around the hotel pool. I looked around at the children, the young parents, all people who we now call our own family, and I cried. We're the oldest people in our church, and John and I have unofficially adopted everyone. They hang out at our house, and when I hear their voices and laughter, I thank God for the extravagant gifts of people and emotions he has put in my life.

I have truly awakened to a life that is messy, adventurous, fun and full of people.

Yellow Brick Roads
The Story of Rachel White
Written by Christee Wise

The small passenger jet bounced and whined down the runway that late summer day. The tunnel, an overgrown accordion, stretched from airport to airplane ready to swallow the three of us. Hydraulics hissed, seatbelts clacked, bells rung and passengers rose. We spilled out into suffocating humidity.

I felt just like the unsuspecting storybook character Dorothy, swept up in a whirlwind and plopped in the Land of Oz.

Indiana was my Oz. No one said it aloud, but clearly we weren't in Palmdale, California, anymore.

Like Dorothy's little Toto, my younger sister Angie and brother Tommy tagged beside and behind me. I drew comfort from their companionship, but also carried a weight of responsibility. Other than this, my luggage was light, our belongings were few. At 16, 15 and 12, we'd only brought what we needed to begin school the next day. Our parents would join us in a couple of weeks, bringing the rest of our pared-down household. Larry and Theresa, the oldest siblings, both had plans to stay in Southern California.

Uncle Mike greeted us cheerfully at the gate. "Welcome to Indiana!"

I forced a smile and allowed a hug.

Resound

My father's brother led us to the second level of the parking garage to his maroon minivan. He unlocked the back door to stow our duffels.

Our family in Indiana made every effort to make us feel at home. Dad would be a bookkeeper at "The Wright Flowers," a shop my Uncle Ron owned. We'd stay with Uncle Ron and Aunt Jayne.

Angie, Tommy and I climbed the spiraling stairway into the loft they'd prepared for us. "The daybed is for you girls," Aunt Jayne explained. She had cleared the closet and thoughtfully provided hangers for each of us. I had borrowed a couple pairs of jeans and a handful of shirts from Theresa when we left, but between us there were few items to put away.

"Thank you," I said simply, my head still spinning with change.

❦ ❦ ❦

Our storm had been brewing for a couple of years. Theresa took time off from college, returned home to work and help with expenses. I had no idea how tight things were at our home in California.

"Rachel, I'm afraid we can't afford to put all of you in private Catholic school anymore," Mother confided. "You're going to have to go to public high school."

My mind absorbed the reality quickly. My heart demanded it, in sensitivity to my parents' pain and sacrifice. I'd just graduated from the eighth grade at St.

Yellow Brick Roads

Mary's, the only elementary school that any of the King children had ever attended. I realized I was not going to be able to attend Paraclete, the high school that my older brother still attended and all my friends were moving on to. I could never admit my jealousy; there was no need.

Surrounded by hundreds of other nervous incoming freshmen, I started public high school two weeks later. Eventually, I made the cheerleading squad and the basketball team. Soon I felt like I belonged at Highland High just as I did in the private school. I was a secure, fresh-faced Dorothy in my happy, wholesome storybook life.

The tornado hit in 1993. The bottom dropped out of the economy in California. A financial funnel cloud swirled up suddenly, twisting and defying prediction, cutting a deadly path through the market and sucking the life out of businesses like my father's real estate company. Dad spent long hours trying to salvage the business. Finally, my papa-daddy approached me one evening that summer, his face shadowed with concern.

He bent down to wrap his arms around me, his petite teenaged daughter preparing for her junior year in high school. "How would you feel about moving back to Indiana close to your uncles and cousins?"

I sensed his agony and stifled my grief.

"Uncle Ron offered me a job at the flower shop, Rachel."

Immediately, I was compelled to justify the move and bury my shock for my father's sake. I searched for a silver lining in the eerie cloud that formed on the horizon of my young life.

I'd still be going to school with Angie and … Chris, our cousin.

A vision of Purdue, the university on which I'd set my sights since middle school, flashed across my mind. My flagging hopes of going to college caught an updraft. *We'll be close to Purdue University; maybe there's a chance of going to college after all.*

Resistance would serve no one, anyway. In emergencies, families come together, they watch out for each other. They hold one another's hands and flee to safety. Dad's breath felt warm on my neck. His hot tears spilled down onto my skin. I held tightly to him and forced myself to be strong.

We didn't have the money for the move. Dad threw out an idea as his own faith was tested. "If we can sell the van for $3,000, then this is what we are to do."

The van sold. We packed. As my friends got ready to go back to Highland, I attended going-away parties and said goodbye too many times. Only my closest friends knew exactly why we were going; we weren't the only ones hit by the downturn.

ॐॐॐ

Where is this school? I wondered dolefully. We'd been driving for 20 minutes in the rural countryside, so different than the suburbs of Southern California.

Yellow Brick Roads

Uncle Ron walked Angie and me into Harrison High and introduced us. The counselor was no taller than me with curly red hair. Her tiny treble voice made her seem almost childlike. She was kind, but asked the same question we would hear over and over. "Ooooh, you're from California," she cooed. "What are you doing here in Indiana?"

I don't know. I should be in California, cheerleading and having a good time with my friends. But Dad's job is here.

Theresa was back at college, and Larry was trying to pursue a career as a California firefighter, staying with friends. The temper tantrum rising inside frightened me. I could never admit how jealous I was of Larry or how desperately I wished I could stay. I buried the dark thoughts and bit my tongue.

Angie and I were assigned different lunch periods. The first two days I ate in the library for fear of sitting in someone's regular spot.

I had never had this problem. I was bubbly and popular and at the center of the activity in my old school. I didn't even know where to begin in this strange place.

What am I doing in this school out here in the cornfields in the middle of nowhere?

I'd always done well in school, but soon discovered the schools in the West were behind those in the Plains states. Students of all grade levels were mixed together, and I couldn't tell who was who. It was a much smaller school, but we were outsiders in every way.

Resound

Angie's fiery personality served her well. Though she had a hard time, she embraced William Henry Harrison High School as her high school for the next three years. Having committed myself so completely to St. Mary's and then to Highland, I couldn't take the risk.

When I discovered a distant cousin, Carmen, I introduced myself and asked if I could sit with her group at lunchtime.

"So …" A perky blonde turned away from me to her friend, after they'd asked me the one burning question they had about California: "Were there gangs in your high school?"

"What happened on *Days*?"

Several minutes into the conversation, I realized that Perky was talking about *Days of Our Lives.*

These girls are totally into soap operas! Gag me!

Mom and Papa-Daddy finally arrived with our things. We all stayed with Uncle Ron and Aunt Jayne for another two months.

On the day we moved into our new place, all five of us slept together on the floor in one of the empty rooms. We were so happy just to be together again. When our furniture was delivered, I buried my face in the couch and breathed the familiar smell of home.

After a while, I came to know Carmen's group and grew to like the girls. They invited me to Young Life, a Christian group for high school students. I was soon attending regularly. Though I liked the other students, the music and activities, I still felt like I was on the outside looking in. My classmates seemed to have a real connection with God that I couldn't grasp.

∾∾∾

Sometimes at Young Life, I thought about my first encounter with God the summer before we moved. Theresa was dating the son of an evangelical pastor after she'd returned to college. My mother allowed us to attend Jonathan's church, Calvary Chapel, sometimes as long as we attended Catholic church with the family on Sundays.

One summer evening, when I was 15, we attended a Harvest Crusade at Dodger Stadium featuring a number of Christian bands. I listened in amazement to several young adults testify that God had revealed himself to them and changed their lives. The enthusiastic crowd stood to their feet and cheered as if the home team had just won the pennant.

"If you feel like Christ is calling you, come down. He loves you, and he wants to meet you right here, tonight," the emcee suggested. Something stirred inside me. We'd never done anything like this in Catholic church. We never talked about "getting saved."

I turned to my sister. "I want to go down."

Thousands of people streamed from the stands and flooded the field. My seat must have been in the farthest section, because it took forever to get down to the infield. I don't know where I went or how I found my group afterward, but I knew that day I had committed my life to

Resound

God and received Christ as my Savior. Soon, I'd be in Indiana, though, looking for a yellow brick road.

෨෨෨෨

The summer after we moved, I returned to California for a visit.

"Mom, I want to stay in California. Please?" I pleaded over the phone. "Kristine's parents say it's okay. Just let me stay here with them." I let my real feelings surface as I begged to go back to the place I so fondly remembered as home.

"Rachel, you need to be here with your family. This is where you belong." Mother was firm.

"Fine," I snapped. "Then can I stay a week longer?"

"All right," she relented. "You can stay one more week, but then you're coming home."

My anger boiled near the surface. *Indiana is not my home. I don't belong there.*

I brought along my sour attitude when I returned.

The culture shock had completely eroded my self-esteem. I had some ongoing medical issues and often felt under the weather. I'd gained weight and was not the same person I was before the move inside or outside my body — and everyone in my family noticed.

"I'm going to try out for cheerleading," Angie told me one day.

Maybe if I try out and make it, I'll get into the swing of things, I mused half-heartedly.

Yellow Brick Roads

The day the results were posted, my little sister could barely contain her excitement. She hurried to the board ahead of me. She stood on her toes, leaned into the huddle of chattering hopefuls, scanned the list and then rocked back slowly and stood upright. A lump formed in my throat. I saw the conflict in her eyes.

"Rachel," she stood like a courageous little protector directly in front of me, "I'm so sorry."

"It's okay, really. Congratulations to you!" I was truly happy she had made it. I knew it would be a highlight of high school for her, as it had been for me. Later, in private, I cried with heartache much deeper than failure to make the team.

I focused on my studies and looked forward to Young Life's service projects. In serving others, I forgot about my own pain and discovered I truly loved people, young, old and in-between.

❧❧❧

My heart was pounding as I stared at the envelope bearing the Purdue logo. Dropping my books on the table, I tore open the letter. Subconsciously, I braced myself for disappointment.

"I got accepted!" I grabbed Tommy's shoulders and shook him. He wobbled, pretending that I knocked him off balance, but his eyebrows and the corners of his mouth lifted merrily. Finally, something happy had happened to me.

Resound

College promised a new start for me. The gloom I felt since moving to Indiana stopped at the edge of the beautiful campus. Trees and bubbling fountains dotted the landscape, permeating the air with sounds of movement and life. Students buzzed around on bikes, gathered in clusters to study or paused to greet each other on the sidewalk. The university atmosphere reminded me of California.

The first year I lived at home, but I took a job as cashier in the cafeteria. Faculty and students both began to recognize me. My confidence grew. Being with people energized me and eased the depression.

Guys were beginning not only to notice me, but to pay attention to me. It made me feel good to make them feel good.

When I went to parties and on dates, I let them touch me and kiss me, even though I hardly knew them. The freedom of being on my own was intoxicating enough, but I started drinking and partying.

I had always liked church as a child, but I stopped going immediately after I turned 18. The brief encounters I'd had with God didn't transfer to handling daily challenges in my life. I imagined I was of little use or interest to a great big holy God. I had been confirmed in the Catholic church as a young teenager and checked the requirement off my list.

My second year, I moved to an apartment on campus and changed my major to Child Development. On my own, I dismissed restraint. I'd always planned to save myself for marriage, but gave up my virginity to an older guy I'd just met at a party. I regretted it terribly later.

Later in the semester, several friends and I were partying apartment to apartment when one gathering began to get out of control. A male student I didn't know became violent, turning on the other party-goers and yelling and throwing things.

Adrian, a sophomore I'd met earlier, urged us down the hall into an empty bedroom. "Don't come out unless I tell you, okay?" he warned.

Down the hall the commotion went on for a long time, with Adrian checking on us periodically. Then everything was quiet, and he came back to release us. "You need to be more careful."

Adrian was a gentleman. He was funny and smart, and I liked being around him.

ॐॐॐ

A dozen monstrous high-voltage snakes danced in front of the windshield. In horror, I clung to the shuddering steering wheel and watched as Adrian's blue Ford Probe catapulted ahead of me. End-over-end Adrian's car flipped, then bounced off a boulder and ricocheted toward a steep drop-off. Suddenly, it slammed against the midsection of a power pole and exploded in a bolt of lightning. The pole splintered into a shower of wooden javelins. The snapping serpents were loosed, and our cars fell 50 feet apart in the midst of a deadly pit.

Resound

Seconds before, my eyes had been drawn to the rearview mirror and Adrian, who was following me in his car from my parents' house back to the university. I stared in surprise as he maneuvered around me at 40 miles per hour on the winding suburban highway. There wasn't enough time or roadway for him to pass safely. A truck sped toward him in the oncoming lane.

Adrian swerved back into our lane clipping my left front fender. For a split second, the white Probe I'd borrowed from my roommate locked with his. We left the roadway together. My head whipped forward as I hit the deep ditch. Instantly, the back window imploded, deluging me with shattered glass. My head jerked back and around, rocking finally into place between my shoulders.

Still, I braced myself with an iron grip on the steering wheel. The borrowed car fell, trembled and died. The scene that unfolded beyond the demolished windshield filled me with a single dreadful thought.

Adrian is dead!

I tumbled from my car and scrambled toward his. Broken power lines gnashed their electric teeth. Blindly, I plunged through the weeds toward Adrian. Like vipers, the cables stung the bodies of both cars leaving blackened welts the size of hubcaps on their hoods and fenders.

Shock. The certainty of Adrian's death concealed the peril of the downed lines. I rushed toward his car. I saw the right side first, completely crushed where any passenger certainly would have been killed. I could not see the driver at all.

Yellow Brick Roads

I stumbled around the car ready to pull Adrian from the wreckage. I saw no movement. Then, his fixed, alarm-filled eyes caught mine, and I froze in my tracks inches from the driver's side window.

"Don't touch the car!" he shouted, and I jumped. "Get away from the car, Rachel!"

My knees went weak, and I dropped to the ground, panting and sobbing, "He's alive. He's alive."

Back on campus and in the surrounding area, lights went out, computers shut down, elevators stopped halfway between floors. Production at the Eli Lilly pharmaceutical manufacturer halted. The accident sent a massive power surge through the grid, and electricity went out all over the county.

I heard sirens, felt a blanket around my shoulders and shivered with cold and fright as I was led back toward the road. My strength and awareness disintegrated. It seemed like hours before Adrian was freed. I refused to go to the hospital and waited in the bitter cold. Instead, I asked for a phone to call my parents and my roommate.

Miraculously, neither of us required paramedics. We huddled in the cab of the ambulance.

"She's going to break up with you, ya'know?" The ambulance driver chuckled at Adrian.

Adrian looked straight into his eyes. "She loves me. She's not going to break up with me." His voice was filled with confidence.

Shivering between them, my heart warmed and melted at the earnestness of Adrian's declaration.

Resound

A few weeks before the accident, Adrian had said, "I love you."

No man had ever said this to me. I was very fond of Adrian, and told him I loved him, too.

Both cars were totaled. Residents of the university were polled to determine damages they'd suffered because of the power failure. As a result, the university assessed a $60,000 bill against Adrian's student account. The outstanding balance, yet unsettled with the insurance company, prevented his enrollment the following school year.

The accident seemed to seal an unbreakable bond between us. We had already bound ourselves together by having premarital sex. After the accident, my fear of losing Adrian escalated.

The burden of responsibility weighed heavily on Adrian. Unable to return to school, he was thrust into jobs that were uninteresting, low-paying and sometimes short-term. Too much of the time, we spent nights together partying and sleeping together.

❧❧❧

Months later, I stared at myself in the bathroom mirror at the house Adrian shared with two other guys.

"I can't believe this is happening to me," I whispered angrily. I waited, pacing back and forth on the linoleum, stopping only to berate myself in the mirror. I picked up the pregnancy test strip. Panic-stricken, I caught myself on the edge of the sink. My legs went weak. "What am I gonna do?"

Purity — one of my beloved parents' most firmly held values — how had I cast it aside so carelessly? Now I was caught. What was I going to tell them? I loved Adrian, but we weren't ready to be parents. "Stupid!" I told myself. "How could you be so stupid?"

I was upset with Adrian. I was upset with God. I was upset with the baby. But I was most upset with myself. I blamed everyone else because of my own guilt-stained conscience. Shame filled every part of my being.

I confided in my sisters only. Then reality set in, and I visited Planned Parenthood in Lafayette. They confirmed the results of the home pregnancy test, and a counselor told me about the services they provided.

"We can provide prenatal care, if you want to have the baby. You can keep it or give it up for adoption. Or you may choose to terminate the pregnancy at our Indianapolis location."

Abortion had not crossed my mind. I had only been thinking about how I would tell my parents and how the course of my life had changed in moments. Along with purity, I'd been taught that life begins at conception and abortion is murder. My parents discussed their views openly and had even participated in some pro-life rallies.

Terminate the pregnancy. I turned the innocuous phrase over in my mind and dismissed it, knowing that it was simply a code for abortion.

My anxiety grew by the hour. In my car, I punched my

own belly and hoped for a miscarriage. "Why are you there? Why?" I yelled at the baby.

Desperately I wished to wake up from the bad dream or turn back the clock and undo what I had done. I wanted to terminate the pregnancy. And the more I thought about it that way, the more I saw an answer to my problem.

Angie begged me to reconsider. "Mom and Dad will understand, Rachel. You made a mistake. Don't get an abortion. They'll forgive you and support you if you have this baby. You know they will."

My ears must have been filled with shame.

I called Planned Parenthood. The nurse told me I'd have to wait four more weeks.

Eight weeks?! I thought miserably but made the appointment.

I could hardly stand to be around my parents because of what I had done and what I was about to do.

"Wow, Rachel, you are so brave to make that choice," a friend commented about my decision.

I wanted to scream. *I'm not brave at all. I'm the biggest chickensh**! This is the chicken way out.*

But the litany of excuses played on in my head. *It's the only way to save face, to get your life back. You can't take care of a baby right now. It wouldn't be fair. For all we know, the baby will be deformed because of all your drinking.*

Adrian drove me to the clinic. I wore baggy clothes and ignored the picketers as I'd been instructed. The building itself was stark and barren. Without trees and landscape, it was lifeless. Adrian was the only guy in the waiting room filled with young girls, myself included, wearing sweats. *They got the letter, too.*

I paid my $324 and waited to hear my name. Adrian wasn't allowed to go back with me.

I sat with others as the staff offered pain meds and an explanation of the process.

A technician took me in for an ultrasound. "… to locate the embryonic tissue. You can watch if you like." This is why they waited until eight weeks, so they could see it … the baby.

I refused to think of it.

Don't look, Rachel. Don't look.

A nurse came in to explain the procedure. "We use an instrument that opens the cervix. This can be painful. You'll feel a gentle suctioning, and it will be over."

"Rachel, get up and run! Get up! Get up and run!" an inner voice shouted.

The doctor came in and introduced himself. "You have a very pretty smile!"

He was almost too pleasant. "Okay, let's get this started."

"Run, Rachel, run!" the voice urged. I was terrified to run and terrified to stay.

The doctor inserted a tool. Excruciating pain shot through my body, radiating from my womb to the tips of my limbs. In a moment, he began to suck the life out of me. Every muscle in my body knotted, and I crushed the nurse's hand with both of mine. All the blood drained from my face, and I believed I was about to die.

What they had taken from me they placed in a jar on the shelf. I knew that was my baby.

The doctor exited, and the nurse returned to set up for the next abortion.

It was over. The problem of pregnancy was solved, and I was free to choose a different road.

But I could not change the fact that, once conceived, that baby was my very first child, and I had taken away its life. My entire being filled with grief and regret. I considered that I might be so lost I'd never find my way home.

A nurse ushered me to a large room lined with numerous recliners all facing the center. "There is juice and crackers to help you get your strength back before you go."

Sickened with pain and shame, I didn't want to face anyone. I wanted to leave that place as soon as possible. I nibbled silently at the cracker and sipped the orange juice.

"That's the worst pain I've ever felt," one said.

"I've had two babies, and that was far worse than giving birth."

"I'm done. I'm out of here. I don't want to be here anymore."

I said nothing.

I said nothing as I left. We walked to the car, and Adrian held the door for me. I slid into the passenger's seat. Before he opened the driver's side, I began to sob.

Yellow Brick Roads

"I'm empty. I just feel so empty," I cried. He pulled me into his arms.

Everywhere I turned, my horrible decision haunted me. A car bearing the hand-painted message "Abortion is murder!" in big letters that dripped fake blood appeared on campus in front of me almost daily.

I'm going to hell. God does not forgive this sin.

My blood ran cold when I heard our debate topic in communications class: *Abortion.*

"They called us names," my dad said proudly when they returned from a pro-life event. My mother prepared a sign bearing the image of my niece, and they stood on a street corner for hours encouraging voters to repeal pro-abortion legislation. I fled the room each time the subject came up, to hide my guilty tears.

Mom observed my withdrawal and asked if I'd been hurt or molested. I lied, told her a partial truth, "There was a guy that got carried away and touched me."

If people only knew what I've done, they wouldn't like me. If my parents knew, they'd stop loving me. God knows. He tried to stop me, but I didn't listen. How could he possibly love or forgive me?

೯ೲೲೲ

Adrian and I defied the odds and stuck together. I finished up at Purdue, landed a great internship and job. Adrian worked hard to finish elsewhere. I admired his tenacity and optimism. His well-planned schemes always included me. We often took long drives, and my shy guy described our future in detail.

Sitting at a stop sign for an unusually long time, his proposal caught me off guard.

"Are you serious?"

He looked confused, then began to search the console for something. Recovering a small jewelry box, he opened it, presented a ring and asked me again.

"I don't believe it! Yes! Of course."

He placed the ring on my trembling finger, and we hugged. My heart soared.

"I'm really sorry that I worried you earlier. I was at your parents' house asking for their blessing. They were talking to me for two hours."

I laughed. I was deeply touched not only by his apology but that he made a point to talk with my parents. I'd been desperate to find him when he was so late, but now I understood.

"I thought it would be quick," he added and then finished with a grin, "and so my car was running in the driveway the whole time."

"For two hours?"

Still grinning, he nodded, and we both laughed. I loved his sense of humor and his thoughtfulness. *He'll make a great husband.*

Having left the church, I wasn't sure where to get married. I thought about going to the justice of the peace.

"Rachel's going to have a pagan wedding," Mother fretted to my aunt.

Yellow Brick Roads

Mother prayed earnestly for me every day of my life. She was disappointed I wasn't attending church, but she never pressured me.

To both our delight, a family acquaintance, Reverend Loren Schaeffer, agreed to counsel us and perform the marriage ceremony. The day of our wedding was the hottest of the year. My hair fell in the blistering heat and humidity, Reverend Schaeffer mispronounced Adrian's name and we forgot to light the candles. But the church was decorated lavishly with flowers from the shop my parents now owned.

Afterward, our friends celebrated and toasted us. Then Papa-Daddy stood and raised his glass. My breath caught. My heart swelled with love for my father.

"My prayer," he began, "is that Rachel and Adrian will both come to know Jesus."

My face grew bright and hot, but I nodded and tipped my glass.

I loved my parents and siblings deeply. I counted on their support and secretly relied upon their prayers. At times, I even asked them to pray, reassuring them that I would one day find my way back to God.

I was certain, when we got married, that I was finally on the right road. Shortly after we were married, I confided to my supervisor at the mental health clinic that I'd had an abortion.

"Rachel, would you like to talk about it with someone?"

I was ready. "Yes, I think so."

Resound

My benefits included sessions with a counselor of my choice, and I found a good fit with Kate. She was a Christian, and after we talked a couple of times, she offered to pray with me. No one had ever prayed for me in this way. Kate spoke of God's love and forgiveness.

Forgiveness. A wish, a hope, a desire awakened in me. Each time I pondered it, I wondered how God could ever forgive me. Could I ever forgive myself?

Unable to sleep one night, I flipped on the computer and Googled the word *forgiveness.* Within seconds, my own name appeared on the screen, "Rachel's Project."

I gasped and clicked on the link. Rachel's Project is a program of the Catholic church for women that have been affected by abortion. Tears filled my eyes as I realized God was trying to tell me he loved me.

Memories of the same voice came rushing back. "Run, Rachel, get out of here!"

I shrunk back in shame knowing I'd heard him calling me away from trouble and refused to listen. No matter how many wrong turns I made, God seemed to know exactly where I was and what I needed at all times.

❧❧❧

We called her Baby White.

My sister Theresa and I took pregnancy tests together and devised a plan to make the announcement as we were gathering in Spokane for Christmas. We waited for the rest of our family at the airport, holding signs decorated as

Yellow Brick Roads

Christmas presents in front of our bellies. "Don't open …"

Emerging from the jet way, they spied and read the signs. We turned the presents around, "… for nine months."

Their faces lit up, and everyone whooped and celebrated.

But something went terribly wrong.

At 12 weeks, the doctor ordered an ultrasound. I called my family, ecstatic that I'd heard the baby's heartbeat for the very first time.

That afternoon, I called back sobbing. Baby White had massive swelling of the brain and stomach.

I recited every Novena and prayer I had learned as a child. I begged God, with whom I'd barely spoken since I was 18, for a miracle. At around 14 weeks, I felt a flutter in my stomach. My prayer had been answered … or my baby was gone.

Adrian sat with me during the second ultrasound. The room was silent except for the periodic clicks of the technician's electronic marker taking measurements. This time, I couldn't tear my eyes from the monitor.

"Here is the baby's head — *click … click.*" The tech spoke quietly. "Here is the baby's stomach — *click … click.* And here …" she hesitated too long, "… is where the baby's heartbeat should be."

"Noooo!" I heard someone moan. Adrian and I crumpled in each other's arms.

The doctor wanted to examine the baby to pinpoint the cause. The torture of labor without promise seemed even crueler than death itself. Angie and Adrian stayed with me.

The nurse brought the baby to me in the tiniest cradle I'd ever seen, barely six inches in length, a two-inch teddy bear nestled beside her. She was wrapped in a flannel blanket the size of a handkerchief and printed all over with pastel hearts. Her skin was nearly transparent making her very, very red. Every feature of a human being was there, though, in miniature, from her nose to arms, fingers, legs and toes.

I learned about the medical causes and effects of Turner's Syndrome and accepted that Baby White was taken for a reason known only to God. Guilt had become my constant companion. *I wonder if God is punishing me. My first was only a few weeks younger than this little one.*

Less than six months later, we'd conceived again. My doctors monitored the baby very closely. Adrian had found work in the Pacific Northwest, and we were preparing to move to Oregon.

The sky was dark, drizzling a steady rain in late fall. Tired from work and 23 weeks pregnant, I wanted to get home. I glanced in the rearview mirror and noted headlights behind me some distance as I pulled up to a stop sign.

Wham! My car slammed forward, and my belly strained at the lap belt. The teenaged driver of the car that hit me burst into tears when she saw I was pregnant. I found myself consoling her while fearing for my own child.

Yellow Brick Roads

Meredith Ann was born on February 18, 2006. She was beautiful and perfect.

Just more than a year later, we were expecting again. The cramping started two weeks after we found out. My heart sank at the sight of blood in the toilet. The doctors feared the worst, as I did, that I was miscarrying. But we could do nothing but wait and see. I enlisted my family to pray.

The bleeding and cramping stopped as quickly as it had begun. Eight months later, we had a beautiful healthy baby boy. We named him Cameron Michael.

❧❧❧

Meredith was an exuberant preschooler and Cameron a busy toddler when the attacks began. I loved being a stay-at-home mom. But asthma and severe allergies kicked up in the summertime. I worried something might happen while Adrian was at work in the evening. What would happen to my little ones if I passed out on the floor?

As I read to the two of them one afternoon in the fall of 2010, I suddenly felt breathless. I couldn't seem to calm myself and thought it was asthma.

The doctor agreed, but as we talked, she detected some anxiety issues. In October I had a follow-up visit.

"What might be causing you to feel so anxious and fearful?" she asked gently. I talked with her about my love and concern for my children.

"You need to have a plan, Rachel, to feel like things are

taken care of if something happened to you." Then she asked, "Have you ever seen a counselor about the anxiety?"

She sat back quietly allowing me time to build my courage. My eyes filled with tears as I confessed that I had indeed talked with someone at one time.

"You don't have to tell me if you don't want to."

"When I was 22, I had an abortion," I confessed, using the word I'd avoided for so long.

Filled with compassion, she looked right into my eyes. "Rachel, I understand," she finished deliberately, "and Jesus forgives you." I was stunned. My medical doctor spoke of God as if we were in church rather than an exam room.

"I know that *they* don't like me to talk with my patients this way," she said carefully. "But I believe that spiritual health and physical health work together. Do you feel like you are safe and okay spiritually? Have you ever asked God to save you?"

Had I not been in Young Life or gone to the crusade when I was a teenager, I'd have had no idea what she was talking about, that being saved meant confessing my sins and asking Jesus into my life. I told her about going forward for prayer.

"Rachel, if you have asked Jesus to save you, you are saved. Just believe that and move forward in your life with that. Ask God to calm you. Ask him. He will do it."

I knew immediately that God was again trying to get through to me. I was ready to listen.

Yellow Brick Roads

I liked Lizanne the moment her husband, Paul, introduced us. Paul, a Jehovah's Witness, had knocked at our door. He and Adrian chatted on our porch. I was eager to talk with anyone who knew anything about God. Lizanne and I soon began meeting weekly to study the Bible. With her encouragement, I dug out my Bible and began to read it for the first time since I was a teenager.

I peppered Lizanne with questions each time we met. Like bright-yellow stepping stones, my friend laid down a rock-solid answer to every question I proposed. Without hesitation, she flipped to a verse in the Bible that corroborated her words. I looked forward to my visits with Lizanne throughout that fall, but I also talked with my brothers and sisters and Mother about some things that were different than I'd learned as a child.

"I'm praying for you, Rachel," Mother promised.

That Halloween, Tommy invited us to a community function hosted by a new church that would be launching in the new year.

Tommy had moved to Hillsboro in 2006 and a year later married a terrific young woman he met at church. We loved having them close by. My little brother had become a strong Christian over the years.

Meredith and Cameron wore their costumes and had a blast bouncing in the big inflatables at "Pump It Up" in Hillsboro. We met several families from the area but could only shrug our shoulders and laugh together at the din of children's joyous shrieks. Pastor Luke of Resound Church introduced himself and spoke briefly to the group.

Resound

"We'll be meeting in the movie theater, and we hope you'll be there for the launch on January 23rd." I could tell that Pastor Luke was from Australia and thought it would be very interesting to go to church in a theater.

I returned to the doctor in November for more breathing treatments. "I notice a change in you," she commented and encouraged me to keep pressing toward God. She was praying for me.

But the panic attacks increased through the holidays. On January 4th, Adrian was forced to call an ambulance. Meredith and Cameron watched in horror as Mommy was taken away to the hospital.

The anxiety came over me in overwhelming waves. Inexplicable fear rose in my chest paralyzing my lungs. "Jesus, help me," I prayed. "Father God, please help me to be calm. Give me peace."

For the next three days, I battled the anxiety by praying. My only hope seemed to be to go directly to God himself and ask for help. Prayer relieved my spirit, and my breathing slowed.

On January 8, 2011, I took several deep breaths in and out and knew without a doubt God had healed me. For the first time, I grasped what it means to have a personal relationship with God. Not only did I hear and respond to him, but he heard and responded to me with his presence and with healing.

We'd made that unmistakable connection I'd seen only in other Christians previously, like my parents, siblings and the Young Life group.

Yellow Brick Roads

This was the kind of direction I needed to find my way out of the spiritual Oz in which I'd wandered.

જ્જજ્જ

I gained a new constant in my life after that and began hearing God with my heart quite often.

Five-year-old Meredith was learning the days of the week. "Mommy, what day is it?"

"It's Monday."

"What do we do on Monday?"

"On Mondays you go to preschool, Tuesdays you stay home … on Sundays, some people go to church."

And so it went every morning until she began to put all of our days in order with designated activities.

"What day is it?"

"It's Sunday, Meredith."

"On Sundays, some people go to church," she concluded matter-of-factly. "But we don't."

"Well, would you like to go to church?"

Her eyes lit up, and her mouth formed a perfect round O. She nodded.

"Do you want to go to Uncle Tommy's church or to Lizanne's church?"

"Uncle Tommy's! I want to see Elijah." Elijah was her cousin.

"What are you guys doing?" Adrian asked curiously.

"We're going to church." I smiled and tipped my chin toward Meredith.

Resound

I was pleasantly surprised when my husband dressed to go with us. Tommy and Casey were surprised to see us. Casey was helping in the children's classes and took Meredith and Cam to see their cousin Elijah.

We sat close to the front to see Tommy playing the guitar on the worship team. Afterward, Adrian and I agreed that it was different than any of the churches we'd ever been to and that we liked it.

I met with Lizanne later that week. Although she spoke of Jesus and God, she said that they were separate and that Jesus was a creation like all of us, rather than one with God as I'd always been taught. My need and respect for Lizanne's friendship rivaled my insecurities about her beliefs.

"I'm so confused," I complained to Adrian. "I think I'm just going to give up on this whole thing. I'm going to stop reading my Bible and forget about it."

Adrian smiled down at me tenderly. "You aren't going to give up."

He knows me too well.

Just before Easter I decided to visit Lizanne's church. I came away sad and empty as they remembered Jesus' death without celebrating his resurrection.

God was speaking to me in a new way. I had to listen with my heart. My firsthand personal experience with the power of Jesus confirmed he was real. Religion was just another yellow brick road. Jesus was the one I needed to follow.

Yellow Brick Roads

જ્જ્જ્

Tears rolled down my face as I raised my hand to acknowledge I needed Jesus to help me find my way home. For almost 20 years, I was displaced and lost. Adrian and I both prayed and asked Jesus into our lives at Resound Church on Easter Sunday 2011.

Suddenly, I was swept up on the gentle winds of God's love and forgiveness. He lifted me out of the confusion of the world, my circumstances and my own understanding about which way to go. Then he carried me on wings of his grace and ever so carefully set me down at home, in the palm of God's hand.

My parents did not know what I had done while I was away, but they did know Jesus and what he could do for me. Their continued prayers helped to bring me home.

We can't help but love our children, even when they fail to listen or they disobey. This is how my heavenly father dealt with me. All along he desired to bring me home, and he made a way through his son Jesus Christ, no matter how many yellow brick roads I tried first. Now they have all faded away, and I have determined to follow only Jesus.

Scrum
The Story of Luke
Written by Arlene Showalter

Air escaped in urgent staccato beats from her lungs as Mum desperately gripped the fingers that wrapped her neck. Gasping through purple lips, she tried prying the hands from their deathly position, trying everything she could with measly half-breaths to free herself from her familiar captor.

But the enraged figure fiercely held his ground, filled with an unexplainable anger that burned for no reason at all. His eyes were wild and vacant, and his knuckles whitened with every breath she took.

Lord, her words nearly echoed through the widening whites of her eyes, *please just protect my boys.*

At age 2, I didn't realize my Mum was nearly strangled to death by the man I called my father.

❧❧❧

After violence had terminated Mum's first marriage, she had stepped with confidence into a relationship with Dad.

His stellar credentials included associate pastor of a vibrant church, and by all accounts from those who knew him, Dad was a "godly" man — one with the ability to even heal others.

Resound

In our hometown in New Zealand, he had one time prayed for God to restore the sight of a man with one glass eye. In a miracle that soon appeared in the local newspaper, the man responded to Dad's prayer with the ability to once again see! Readers were baffled, and the community was stumped. Those in the church viewed his miracles as just that — healings from a man who was obviously following a powerful God.

Husband and father, pastor and friend, the dynamic man successfully lived two lives, public and private — very, very private.

While serving as a pillar of the church, married and fathering three sons, Dad's secret life had included fraternizing in massage parlors and tripping on drugs.

And then, the year I turned 2, attempting to murder my mum.

Dad was one of four men who entered and exited my brothers' and my lives like busy shoppers through a retail revolving door. With men like these, my brothers, my mum and I quickly learned to bind together.

We conducted life like we played our favorite sport. We were a rugby team. Rugby plays require an extreme level of teamwork. For example, during a *scrum*, the eight forwards of one team *bind on*, meaning they wrap an arm around their mates, even grabbing the jersey on the other side to make a tight connection, and press together as one being, pushing against the eight forwards of the opposing team. This takes a great deal of skill, strength, timing and, most importantly, teamwork.

Scrum

Mum and her four boys were that scrum-forming team. With every crisis we "bound on," bound together and forged forward like the strong single unit we knew we'd have to be.

❧❧❧

"Boys, this is Steve." Mum introduced us to the tall man by her side. It had been two years since Dad had fled the family — time that offered us a chance to grow even closer to the woman who held us all together. All of us would have done anything to see her smile. "Steve, this is Paul, my eldest, and David and Luke." She grinned. "We're getting married!"

Understanding escaped my 4-year-old mind, but Mummy's happiness spilled across her three sons. We loved him for loving her.

But behind the roses and chivalry lurked a brutal beast. Not long after the marriage, Steve began beating my older brothers, 7-year-old Paul and 5-year-old David, with a broom.

And he beat Mum. She put up with it because flowers, soft music and apologies always followed the tattoo of fists. And, along with the bruises, Steve gave Mum her fourth son.

One day we found Mum poured out on the kitchen floor, beaten and weeping. My child's heart churned with anger and bewilderment. *How can this loving man turn into such a raving monster?*

Resound

Mum clung to the marriage for the loving side of him and dodged the violent side until the day she came home unexpectedly. Dropping her handbag on the kitchen table, she moved down the hallway, her high-heeled shoes clicking her progress.

She opened the bedroom door.

There lay her husband, Steve, with another woman.

With a shriek, Mum yanked a shoe from her foot, dashed to his side of the bed and scored a heel into his temple.

Mum's third marriage ended after that trip to the hospital.

He deserved that, I thought.

࿇࿇࿇

With all the fake and faithless men who had joined and betrayed our family, Mum decided it was important that we meet a man we could trust. In the absence of a stable physical father in our lives, she deliberately surrounded us with strong male role models, taught us about the value of integrity and introduced us to a man she knew would never cheat, lie or kill.

I was sitting on my bunk after dinner, playing with a transformer toy the night Mum came in for a chat.

"How's it going, son?" she asked, sitting next to me and draping an arm about my shoulders.

"Okay," I said, hands busy changing my superhero to a truck and back again.

"You like that toy?" she asked.

"Yes," I responded, eyes glowing. "It's so super cool how it changes."

"Meeting Jesus is like that," she said. "I was a mess before I met him, especially in my heart. See how your toy changes from one thing to something completely different?"

I nodded.

"That's how it was when I met Jesus. I was so angry and confused, tripping on drugs, trying to find my way in life." She paused.

"One day I was walking to a dealer's to get more drugs. A street preacher stopped me and started telling me things about myself nobody else knew. I freaked out."

Her shoulders lifted. "How could this stranger know these things? I told him to go away. But that night, Jesus came to me, in all my mess." She smiled.

"I experienced his total love. He transformed me. I gave my whole heart to him right then and there. That means I made a decision that I wanted to stop living for me and start living for him. I'll never stop loving him."

Mum's eyes lit up, and I could almost see the physical change in her demeanor when she talked about her life after an introduction to Jesus.

"I want to do that, too," I told her.

"You want to give Jesus your heart?"

"Yes, Mummy."

"And have him change you from one thing to another?"

Resound

I nodded again. Even at that young age, I sensed my mummy had a special, special relationship with Jesus. She was different from most people I knew, and I wanted what she had.

"Well, Luke, let's just ask Jesus into your heart, right now."

"I'm ready, Mummy."

ⸯⸯⸯⸯ

Between her duties as single mother and family team captain, Mum ran a successful greenhouse business in Auckland.

When I was about 9, she felt she needed a break and arranged for Jane, a trusted friend, to watch her four sons while she vacationed on one of New Zealand's many islands with another friend.

"Come on, boys," Jane called. "Let's go for a ride. I'm going to teach Mary how to drive."

The two women sat in the front seat with Paul and me in the back. Dave and Matty sat and played in the rear compartment of the station wagon. Nobody wore seat belts.

Passing through an intersection, Mary hit the accelerator rather than the brake. The car hit a pole. Matty and Dave were thrown against the back seat but suffered no injuries. A screaming ambulance rushed Paul and me to the hospital.

Because I was covered in blood, the nurses frantically

Scrum

snipped away all my clothes. They soon discovered my nose was the source of most of the blood. In addition, I suffered a minor concussion.

Before my discharge, nurses wheeled Paul in and parked his gurney next to mine.

"Hey, Paul, what's going on?" I asked.

He looked at me with a strange, vacant look, totally unresponsive to my question. A short time later, the doctors delivered their somber verdict: Paul had suffered major brain damage.

Someone telephoned Mum, and she returned on the earliest flight. Within minutes, she stormed the waiting room, filled with stunned family and friends, and took command.

"My Jesus has never failed me yet," she declared, "and he's not going to now." She led the entire group into fervent, believing prayer.

In the midst of this storming-heaven's-gates-power-charged prayer, I looked up and saw Paul sauntering down the hall toward us.

My jaw dropped. I looked at Mum. I looked back at Paul.

Nurses and doctors poured into the waiting area, voices bubbling in a hubbub of disbelief, how-is-it-possible amazement ... and joy.

Mum's right, I knew right then. *Jesus never fails.*

ॐॐॐ

Resound

Mum's business grew as fast as her well-tended plants. She needed a sitter for her younger sons and hired an older teenager named Adam.

We got on well with Adam until the day he dropped his pants in front of me.

"Have a look on this," he said.

"Uh, no thanks," I replied, scooting toward the door.

"Come back here!" he yelled.

I ran as fast as a blindside winger with the shed behind our house as my goal. I didn't stop until I reached the safety of the roof. I perched there, waiting for my mum to come home.

Adam's corpulence kept him on the ground.

"Son, why are you up there?" Mum called up to me.

I hollered down my story. She called the cops. They came and removed the perp.

"It's your fault! It's your fault!" Adam screamed as they led him away.

Mum put an arm around me after I shimmied back to earth.

"He's lying, Luke. You did nothing wrong."

Thank you, God, he didn't lay a finger on me.

ৡৡৡৡ

"I've spent far too much time away from you boys," Mum said. "I'm going to sell my business so I can be with you."

When the money ran out from the sale, we descended

Scrum

from comfort to want, but that didn't shake Mum's faith, not in the least. Need pulled us even closer as a team.

One day we sat in an empty kitchen, at a table devoid of food.

"Sons, it's time for a family meeting," Mum said, "to pray for food. What shall we pray for?"

"I want burger rings!" exclaimed 7-year-old Matty. This is a sort of chips in New Zealand.

We each expressed what sort of food we wanted.

"And Pickles needs cat food," Paul added.

After our prayer time, Mum went out to check the mailbox. A stranger pulled up in her car.

"I don't know why I'm here," the lady began, "because you don't look like you are in need, but …"

Mum never looked needy. Neither did her sons.

"God impressed upon me to buy food," the woman continued. "And cat food. I don't even have a cat!"

She handed the package to Mum and drove off. Matty's burger rings sat on top.

Jesus gives specific answers to specific prayers, I mused as I munched on our God-delivered meal. *Jesus must be real.*

❧❧❧

"Did you hear that noise last night?" Matty asked. Due to our reduced income, the new neighborhood wasn't the best, and we were always hearing suspicious noises.

Paul, the eldest at 12, called a team huddle. "We need

to find a way to protect ourselves from possible burglars," he began.

"Yeah, we'd be an easy mark," remarked 10-year-old Dave. "People gotta know Mum's the only parent here."

"Let's rig something up," I suggested.

"With trip wires," Dave added.

"And lots of noise," Matty put in.

We created an elaborate alarm system by running wires to the stereo and more to a box of spoons and various other obstacles.

One night the spoons crashed, and the stereo blared. We all flew out of bed while Mum called the cops. An intruder was caught.

We were too excited to be scared. Our system worked!

What did the intruder tell the cops? "I knew it was a single-parent home with young children. I thought it an easy hit."

Mum's team: 1. Perpetrator: 0.

৵৵৵৵

We loved life. Mum gave us full freedom for boyish creativity. We carved up our backyard into obstacle courses. We rigged up swings high enough to touch heaven.

Paul and I joined the scouts. When I was 10, the organization held a world jamboree in New Zealand. Tents from diverse countries marched with precision across a massive field. Australia's representatives camped

Scrum

next to New Zealand's. Our mum came along to cook and clean during the event.

She met a scoutmaster — a super nice guy named Geoff who owned his own truck and drove for a transportation company ... in Australia.

He showed a genuine interest in Mum's sons.

She introduced him to Jesus.

He returned to Australia.

She went to visit.

He proposed.

She accepted.

"Guess what, boys," Mum said upon her return, eyes as bright as her hair. "I'm going to marry Geoff, and we'll all live in Australia."

My heart sank.

Australia! Is she nuts? What about our friends here? Australia is so big ... and hot ... and strange! And they'll be teasing us, calling us Kiwis and all.

Then I remembered ... Paul's healing ... God's provision ... God's protection.

If God provided for us in New Zealand, he must be able to provide for us in Australia, too.

వావావా

We boys settled into Australian life like pebbles sinking into a pond. Soon we wondered what we'd ever liked about New Zealand. We made friends, swam, played rugby and loved life.

Resound

About a year later, Mum worked at renovating the house while Geoff was at work. Paul and I heard a piercing scream moments before Mum dashed from their bedroom.

"Luke! Paul!" Mum screamed. Her hair splashed about her face like red paint as she flew past us to scoop up my baby brother, Matty.

She flung open the back door. "David, get in here — now!"

Mum bounced from one room to another. "I can't believe it, I can't." The sobbing increased. "Hurry, hurry!" she coaxed. "We have to go."

I made a mad dash for our bedrooms, scooping up whatever my 5-year-old arms could carry, while Mum tugged at my shirt, urging us to the door.

"Come on," she cried, snatching up her keys and purse. "We have to get out of here …"

The four of us huddled in the car, each embracing his few treasures, while Mum mashed the accelerator and drove — as crazy as her words.

She drove us to her friend's home, where she blubbered her news.

"Geoff's a … Geoff's a …" she cried, hands to her face. Her bright red hair swung from side to side as she shook her head.

"A what?" Trish asked.

"He's a pedophile," she wailed.

A what? My mind raced. Geoff had never touched us — not one of us. We were shocked that this kind scoutmaster could have done anything to another child.

"How do you know?" Trish asked.

"I was clearing out our bedroom to paint," Mum began. "I found a box and started looking through the files." She wrung her hands. "I can't believe it, I can't believe it."

"You're sure?" Trish asked.

"Yes, the police records were all there," she wailed. "Oh my, oh my."

We dashed back to New Zealand, but none of us was happy. That one year in Australia had spoiled us. We all wanted to go back.

So we did.

Mum enrolled in the social system for assistance. She also took cleaning jobs and later on she became a masseuse, a good one. Money issues melted away.

Through it all, Mum used the experience to teach us where we needed to place our trust — and it wasn't in any one man we could see.

We grew stronger, we built our scrum and our family team got on with life.

My father's mother came to visit us in Australia when I was 12. We had a blast, showing Grandma our new life and world. Grandma loved us all, with total, unconditional love. She loved Matty as much as her three biological grandsons.

Not long after her departure, Grandma sat down to write a letter to us. At that moment, she suffered a heart attack and died.

Resound

She left each of us, including Matty, equal portions in her inheritance, set aside for our education.

Shortly after that, the phone rang. Mum spoke to my father for the first time since he'd tried to kill her 10 years before.

"You give me the whole inheritance," he growled over the phone, "or I'll hire a hit man."

Mum called a family huddle and gave our team the rundown so we could make our next play. "Your father has threatened my life," she explained. "But I feel it is an empty threat. I'm not scared." She smiled. "I'm not giving him the money. Are you all with me on this?"

"Sure, Mum," we all chorused.

We all knew that if God could protect us from a perpetrator, he could certainly protect us from our father.

৵৵৵

We never felt cheated without a permanent father in our lives. Mum had taught us too well that God is the ultimate father. We trusted her … and God on that.

"Always remember, boys," she'd say, "life is an adventure." We embraced her assurance with all our boyish hearts and zeal. We could hardly wait for the next adventure and often found it closer to home than expected.

Mum was deliberate about exposing us to wise and seasoned elders — people who would lead by example in the ways our own fathers could not.

Scrum

One couple made it their passion to love us and lead us down the right, not just the easy, paths. Fred, a retired pastor, and his wife, Dorothy, took us boys into their hearts and home. And they gently and lovingly mentored us the way our own fathers didn't.

One day, Fred heard Paul telling a dirty joke.

"Come here, boys," he said to the four of us, his voice kind and fatherly.

"Let me explain to you what a real man is." In his own gentle way, he explained integrity, honor, purity and how important it is to love God with all we are and have.

Fred lived what he taught. I respected him and learned.

This is what it looks like to be a man and lead a family, I thought. I noted his example and stored it subconsciously in the back of my memory.

॰॰॰॰

Crouch … touch … pause … *Engage!* Adrenalin surged from my toes to my fingertips as my body strained forward. The moment the scrum half had possession of the ball, I broke out of formation and dashed into play.

Eighty minutes of unadulterated joy flooded my 15-year-old body as I played the sport that had become both my hobby and my family life. The love of rugby pulsated with every heartbeat and oxygenated my every breath.

A few hours later, I flopped, tired but contented, on my bunk and picked up my Bible. Rugby players and Aussie racing cars sped across my walls in bright posters.

Resound

Kaleidoscopic thoughts wove themselves in my head as I read. *Life is great,* I mused. *I'm young and strong, and today I got to play breakaway, the coolest position in rugby. Matty and I play on the same worship team, there are lotsa pretty girls at school, Mum's work is good ...*

A new thought, or sensing, crept into the whirlwind assessment.

Luke, I want you in ministry.

My heart stopped ... then pounded. Was God speaking to me? And did he want me in ministry? *Young people don't do ministry. It's an unpaid position. How could I support myself?*

The sense stayed ... and grew.

My mother wandered into the room.

"Mum," I said, "I think maybe God is calling me into ministry. What do you think?"

Mum's relationship with God was so real. It seemed she held a continuous conversation with the one man who had always been there for her, and I respected her opinion in matters like these.

"Well, Luke, just sit on it, and wait for confirmation." She leaned against the door and crossed her arms. "Allow God to speak to you, and if you're really hearing God, you'll know."

Two days later, a guest speaker came to our church. When he pulled me aside, I knew I wasn't the only one hearing this calling.

"Son," he told me, "I believe God is calling you into ministry."

Scrum

Two weeks later, another person said the same thing. For 12 months, God sent messenger after messenger to confirm what I felt in my heart: He wanted me in ministry.

ॐॐॐ

Because of her own dysfunctional and abusive background, Mum preferred to leave unpleasant situations rather than face them head on. She moved as often as she changed her shoes. When I was 17, she asked us to do it again.

"I'm done with moving," I protested.

"Think of it as a new adventure," she coaxed.

"Not this time, Mum," I said. "It's my last year of high school, and I want to finish with my chums."

She shrugged. "How will you do it?" she asked.

"I'll get a room," I said. "I need to stay." I wanted the stability of staying in one place long enough to establish myself. So I stayed in Canberra, applied for government assistance and found a room to rent. It took me one and a half hours to get to school each day, but it was so worth it.

The sense that God wanted me in ministry had never left me. But I felt I needed a breather after high school and took a year off. I supported myself waiting tables. Surely, ministry could wait a short summer or two.

I scraped together enough money to buy my first car, which I proceeded to drive like the Aussie racers I admired so much.

Resound

My best friends, Ben and Woodie, and I hung out together, talking about girls and fast cars. And we talked to God about our futures.

We camped together, chilled at the beach and had good, clean, albeit not always safe, fun.

"Hey, guys," Woodie said. "How about making a potato gun?"

"Sounds cool," Ben and I echoed.

We scrambled to assemble the proper PVC pipe and couplers, flint igniter, hair spray, cement and a sack of potatoes. After sawing, drilling, filing and cementing, we had a real spud launcher … and a blast.

When the year was up, I moved on to Sydney and enrolled in Bible college.

"Hey," I said to a fellow student, who could pass for my twin. "Name's Luke, what's yours?"

"Luke."

We both grinned and formed a friendship that lasts to this day. I often visited Luke's home, where I met his father, Pastor John McMartin. He took me in as a second son named Luke.

He took his two Lukes fishing, mentored me like a spiritual father and allowed me to see the good, the bad and the ugly of him, freely sharing his whole life with me.

Pastor John taught me what a real man is … and does.

Halfway through my two-year course, I received an unexpected phone call while I was cleaning the youth storage closet at Hillsong Church.

Scrum

"Luke, this is Mum."

"Hi, Mum."

"I've some bad news for you," she began.

My heart pounded. Vague, formless thoughts careened through my mind. "Who ... what ..."

"Ben, your childhood friend, was killed in an auto accident," she said. "In Melbourne."

I stood stunned, speechless. *Ben? The fellow who could ditch any cop? Negotiate his way out of any situation?* My thoughts raged. *How, how?*

"He was teaching his girlfriend, Angel, how to drive," Mum explained. "She rolled the car."

There, alone in the storage cabinet, I wrestled and prayed.

This makes no sense to me, God. My mind recalled all the stupid things we'd done as kids. None of those things had killed us.

As I wept and prayed, anger against Angel rose up. I quashed it. I couldn't blame her for an event God allowed.

I didn't blame God, either. But, at 18, life seemed much shorter. And I knew I couldn't hide from my calling while waiting tables and taking a breather from the real calling in my life.

From this moment on, Lord, I'm more determined than ever to pour out my life for Jesus. Ben knows I don't have any time to waste.

❧❧❧

Resound

I faced graduation from Bible college with some trepidation. *Nobody hires kids for pastorate jobs.*

But God had my back. I was offered a job at Canberra Life Center as a youth pastor. I took it.

Who am I, I thought, sitting at a state meeting, surrounded by older, more experienced pastors, *and what am I doing here?* At 19, I was the youngest youth pastor in the country. I felt as though every eye there bore through me.

Thoughts of inadequacy tried to slap me down.

"I'll just stick it out," I decided. "And see what God wants me to do."

❧❧❧

As it turned out, he had a lot in store.

"Hi." The slender beauty with bright bluish-green eyes greeted me. "My name's Alissa."

She's cute.

I learned she'd just returned from England after touring Europe. I learned other interesting facts as we hiked together, played sets of tennis or enjoyed chats at local cafes.

She's got a sweet spirit, I thought as I got to know her better. *But I want to take it slow. Let's build a good friendship first.*

Nine months passed. *I dig this girl. I love her creativity and her beautiful smile … I'm gonna ask her to marry me!*

I made arrangements for Friend A to pick her up for

dinner in Canberra. At least, that's what Alissa thought. Friend A handed Alissa a one-way ticket to Sydney and drove her to the airport.

After the short flight, Friend B picked her up and drove her to a lovely restaurant, located under a bridge.

Alissa arrived, eyes huge with bewilderment, especially at the sight of me in a suit.

I grinned.

"Look at that boat," I said, pointing at the water.

She turned. Friend C motored by, with a gigantic sign hanging from the side of his boat. Huge love hearts encircled the words *Will you marry me?*

Alissa read the sign and turned back … to find me on bended knee, grinning and holding up a ring.

"Yes!" she cried.

We enjoyed a nice dinner, then I drove her to Canberra, discussing wedding plans on the three-hour trip back.

Alissa moved to Sydney after our wedding. I felt my time as a youth pastor was finished and discussed it with Pastor John.

"How about working for me," he asked, "as a young adult pastor? Give it two years, and then I'm sure God will tell you the next step."

"Sounds good to me," I agreed.

Alissa made good money as an interior designer. I enjoyed my work.

Then the familiar sense returned. I had met a pastor from Cedar Rapids, Iowa, Larry Sohn, and we became good friends. He invited me to check out the United States.

"I'd like to take you to lunch," I told Alissa one day.

"That would be nice," she agreed.

We drove to downtown Sydney.

"This opportunity has arisen," I explained over our meal, "with Larry. He wants us to fly out — no strings attached — for a visit."

Alissa nodded.

"He thinks we're supposed to move to the States."

She nodded again.

A week later, we flew to Iowa. At first it seemed so backward, not at all our style of a city.

But we felt peace — immeasurable, unfathomable, unexplainable peace. We knew that this kind of peace could only come from God.

"This would be a good place to raise a family," Alissa said.

I agreed.

We made the move and immersed ourselves into the American culture. I soon recognized one vast difference between the two cultures: In Australia, folks go to church only if they want to. But here in the States, we've met many, many Americans who go to church, but don't know *why*. And so they miss out on the reality of life with Jesus.

Not long after our move to the States, I experienced the urge to find my biological father, whom I'd not seen or spoken to in years.

"Where's Daddy?" I would ask Mum frequently

throughout my younger years. She'd gather me in her arms and hold me tight.

"I'll explain," she'd say, "when you're older."

Mum never hid life from her sons.

"You're old enough now," she had told us one day. "Sit here." She patted the spot on the sofa next to her. "And I'll tell you what happened to your daddy."

I sat down. She wrapped an arm around me, and she told me the story of how Jesus saved her life the day he sent the next-door neighbor boy to her house as my father attempted to kill her when I was only 2 years old.

"Just as I felt darkness covering me, I cried in my spirit, 'God, look after my three boys.' At that very moment, the kid next door walked in the front door.

"'Sir,' he cried, 'what are you doing?' Your father bolted for the door. We never saw him again." She paused, being very specific and deliberate with her next words.

"Boys," she'd said, "that boy had never been in our home before." The realization of what that meant slowly sunk in, and the God I was just learning to trust as my real father became even more real.

There was no other time the child had ever been to our house. And yet, in the midst of one random moment on one random day that would have ended Mum's life and changed ours forever, a boy mysteriously appeared. Out of nowhere. For no good reason.

"God sent him — and saved my life," Mum said.

God loved his children enough to send a child to intercede on their behalf. Just as my earthly father sought to bring about death, the father who never failed sent someone to bring about life.

I leaned back in my chair, remembering the fierceness of her hug that day. *As always, God,* I thought, *you proved your faithfulness by answering Mum's prayer.*

I leaned forward and Googled Dad's name, hoping to find him and share how full and satisfying my own life was. I found him — everywhere — and read article after article, courtesy of the Internet. *Behind bars for attempted murder.* He was a former pastor, an amazing speaker, a man documented in local newspapers for healing the *blind* — and he had stabbed a man in the *eye.* I shook my head — not in anger, nor shame — but with sadness.

My dad had never defined me, nor had I needed him to fulfill me. Although my mum had failed to find a quality soul mate for her own life, she excelled bringing other souls to Jesus.

I smiled. *She's always been a spiritual pillar to me. Thank you, Lord, for such a mother!*

My thoughts returned to my father, whose bad choices had removed him from ministry. It was no coincidence that I was the offspring of a fallen minister and now myself serving in ministry.

The world would call it ironic; I would call it something only God could do.

The next year, God blessed us with a precious daughter and two years after that, a second daughter. I love being what my father never was … a real daddy.

Scrum

❧❧❧

God called us to move again.

"I feel God wants me to plant a church," I confided in my friend Benny. "But ..." I hesitated.

"Hasn't God supplied your need every other time?" he asked. "Why not now?"

His words encouraged me to proceed. After a long period of prayer, God clearly showed us he wanted us to go to Oregon.

Seven of us moved out west and started telling people about Jesus — just like my mum — anytime, anywhere.

We found hungry, searching souls in Starbucks and at the hairdressers. On the streets and at the mall. People began pouring into our home like fans at a rugby match. They filled our couches and lined our countertops.

Churches began offering us the use of their buildings. Less than a year after our move, in January 2011, we launched Resound Church with 360 people.

We didn't come to offer people another church option. We came to love on them.

We came to show them Jesus in action. We roll up our sleeves and get our hands dirty, working anywhere and everywhere there is a need. We show those with hurts, habits and hang-ups that, despite their past, despite their family history, despite their experiences with an earthly mother or an earthly father, the ultimate father came to love them, to save them and to give them abundant life.

Conclusion

My heart is full. When I became a pastor, my desire was to change the world. My hope was to see people encouraged and the hurting filled with hope. As I read this book, I saw that passion being fulfilled. However, at Resound, rather than being content with our past victories, we are spurred to believe that many more can occur.

Every time we see another changed life, it increases our awareness that God really loves people, and he is actively seeking to change lives. Think about it: How did you get this book? We believe you read this book because God brought it to you seeking to reveal his love to you. Whether you're a man or a woman, an engineer at Intel or a barrista, blue collar or no collar, a parent or a student, we believe God came to save you. He came to save us. He came to save them. He came to save all of us from the hellish pain we've wallowed in and offer real joy and the opportunity to share in real life that will last forever through faith in Jesus Christ.

Do you have honest questions that such radical change is possible? It seems too good to be true, doesn't it? Each of us at Resound warmly invite you to come and check out our church family.

Freely ask questions, examine our statements and see if we're "for real" and, if you choose, journey with us at whatever pace you are comfortable. You will find that we are far from perfect. Our scars and sometimes open wounds are still healing, but we just want you to know God is still completing the process of authentic life change in us. We still make mistakes in our journey, like everyone will. Therefore, we acknowledge our continued need for each other's forgiveness and support. We need the love of God just as much as we did the day before we believed in him.

If you are unable to be with us, yet you intuitively sense you would really like to experience such a life change, here are some basic thoughts to consider. If you choose, at the end of this conclusion, you can pray the suggested prayer. If your prayer genuinely comes from your heart, you will experience the beginning stages of authentic life change, similar to those you have read about.

How does this change occur?

Recognize that what you're doing isn't working. Accept the fact that Jesus desires to forgive you for your bad decisions and selfish motives. Realize that without this forgiveness, you will continue a life separated from God and his amazing love. In the Bible, the book of Romans, chapter 6, verse 23 reads, "The result of sin (seeking our way rather than God's way) is death, but the gift that God freely gives is everlasting life found in Jesus Christ."

Believe in your heart that God passionately loves you and wants to give you a new heart. Ezekiel 11:19 reads, "I will give them singleness of heart and put a new spirit

Conclusion

within them. I will take away their stony, stubborn heart and give them a tender, responsive heart" (NLT).

Believe in your heart that "if you confess with your mouth that Jesus is Lord and believe in your heart that God raised him from the dead, you will be saved" (Romans 10:9 NLT).

Believe in your heart that because Jesus paid for your failure and wrong motives, and because you asked him to forgive you, he has filled your new heart with his life in such a way that he transforms you from the inside out. Second Corinthians 5:17 reads, "When someone becomes a Christian, he becomes a brand new person inside. He is not the same anymore. A new life has begun!"

Why not pray now?

Lord Jesus, if I've learned one thing in my journey, it's that you are God, and I am not. My choices have not resulted in the happiness I hoped they would bring. Not only have I experienced pain, I've also caused it. I know I am separated from you, but I want that to change. I am sorry for the choices I've made that have hurt myself, others and denied you. I believe your death paid for my sins, and you are now alive to change me from the inside out. Would you please do that now? I ask you to come and live in me so that I can sense you are here with me. Thank you for hearing and changing me. Now please help me know when you are talking to me, so I can cooperate with your efforts to change me. Amen.

Resound

Portland's unfolding story of God's love is resounding here in the Hillsboro and Beaverton area … can you hear your name vibrating with it?

I hope to see you this Sunday!

Luke Reid
Resound Church
Hillsboro, Oregon

We would love for you to join us!

We meet Sunday mornings at 9 and 10:15 a.m. at
Regal Cinema Evergreen Parkway
2625 NW 188th, Hillsboro, OR 97205

26/NW Sunset Hwy

NW 185th Ave

NW Evergreen Pkwy

Lead Pastor Luke Reid
Phone: 503.724.1688
E-mail: luke@resoundchurch.com

Youth & Children's Pastor Jordan Smalley
Phone: 503.894.2497
E-mail: jordan@resoundchurch.com

www.resoundchurch.com

Mailing Address
P.O. Box 5752
Beaverton, OR 97007

Christmas Eve at the Crystal

SATURDAY DECEMBER 24 2011

6:00PM

1332 W. BURNSIDE
PORTLAND, OR 97209

JOIN US FOR OUR CHRISTMAS EVE SERVICE
WITH PROGRAMS FOR PRE K CHILDREN
AND FOOD CATERED BY MCMENAMINS

WWW.RESOUNDCHURCH.COM

FOR MORE INFORMATION CALL 503.547.9396
OR EMAIL LUKE RESOUNDCHURCH.COM

For more information on reaching your city with stories from your church, please contact Good Catch Publishing at www.goodcatchpublishing.com

GOOD CATCH PUBLISHING

Did one of these stories touch you?
Did one of these real people move you to tears?
Tell us (and them) about it on our reader blog at
www.goodcatchpublishing.blogspot.com.